Marketing of Olympic Sport Organisations

Alain Ferrand
and
Luiggino Torrigiani

Master Exécutif en Management des Organisations Sportives,
Executive Masters in Sports Organisation Management

**HUMAN
KINETICS**

Library of Congress Cataloging-in-Publication Data

Ferrand, Alain.
  Marketing of Olympic sport organisations / Alain Ferrand, Luiggino Torrigiani.
      p. cm.
  Includes bibliographical references.
  ISBN 0-7360-5930-X (soft cover)
  1. Sports--Societies, etc.--Marketing. 2. Sports administration. 3. Olympics--Management. I. Torrigiani,
Luiggino, 1962- II. Title.
  GV716.F47 2005
  338.4'379648--dc22

                                        2004022804

ISBN-10: 0-7360-5930-X
ISBN-13: 978-0-7360-5930-5

The Web addresses cited in this text were current as of November 4, 2004, unless otherwise noted.

Acquisitions Editor: Myles Schrag; **Developmental Editor:** Amanda S. Ewing; **Copyeditor:** Joyce Sexton; **Proofreader:** Bethany J. Bentley; **Permission Manager:** Dalene Reeder; **Graphic Designer:** Nancy Rasmus; **Graphic Artist:** Dawn Sills; **Photo Manager:** Kelly J. Huff; **Cover Designer:** Keith Blomberg; **Photographer (cover):** © Getty Images; **Art Manager:** Kelly Hendren; **Illustrator:** Al Wilborn; **Printer:** United Graphics

Printed in the United States of America   10   9   8   7   6   5   4   3   2

Human Kinetics
Web site: www.HumanKinetics.com

United States: Human Kinetics
P.O. Box 5076
Champaign, IL 61825-5076
800-747-4457
e-mail: humank@hkusa.com

Canada: Human Kinetics
475 Devonshire Road Unit 100
Windsor, ON N8Y 2L5
800-465-7301 (in Canada only)
e-mail: orders@hkcanada.com

Europe: Human Kinetics
107 Bradford Road
Stanningley
Leeds LS28 6AT, United Kingdom
+44 (0) 113 255 5665
e-mail: hk@hkeurope.com

Australia: Human Kinetics
57A Price Avenue
Lower Mitcham, South Australia 5062
08 8277 1555
e-mail: liaw@hkaustralia.com

New Zealand: Human Kinetics
Division of Sports Distributors NZ Ltd.
P.O. Box 300 226 Albany
North Shore City
Auckland
0064 9 448 1207
e-mail: info@humankinetics.co.nz

Contents

Foreword

The work you are about to discover is the second in the MEMOS collection following *Strategic and Performance Management of Olympic Sport Organisations,* published in 2004. MEMOS is a high-level training programme for managers of Olympic organisations. It permits them to obtain an executive Masters degree in the management of sport organisations, issued by the University of Lyon, France, and co-organised by a network of European universities and schools of sport*.

In 2005, the MEMOS programme will celebrate its 10th anniversary—and it has come a very long way since the beginning! The original idea, and one that is still highly valid today, was for the Olympic movement and academic institutions to collaborate in creating a form of teaching that established the link between theory and practice within sport management. This idea immediately won the support of the International Olympic Committee (IOC) President at the time, Juan Antonio Samaranch, and the Director of Olympic Solidarity, Pere Miró. It was also backed by the European Olympic Committees, presided at the time by Jacques Rogge, the current IOC President. We take this opportunity to express our sincere thanks to them.

Despite these highly prestigious supporters, success did not come about immediately, as is often the case for original ideas that require some fine-tuning. I remember one meeting in Lyon with Jean Camy, the founder and first director of MEMOS, and Alain Ferrand, one of the authors of this work. At that meeting, we concluded that we needed to change everything except the name, MEMOS, which was already perceived as a brand, and to use a concept that is developed in the chapters to follow. I took over as the head of MEMOS in 1999 and led it to evolve from a European Masters to an Executive Masters, without changing the French acronym for the title: Executive (European) Masters in the Management of Sport Organisations. In fact, we were already enrolling more and more executives from the national and international sports federations and Olympic Committees from throughout the world. Since the beginning, we have trained more than 200 managers from five continents in the intricacies of Olympic sport management. Today, these graduates constitute a network of expertise and a learning community that are unique. In 2005, the graduates from the eighth edition of MEMOS will join this community—the first course to have benefited from a series of manuals published by Human Kinetics, one of the leading publishers in this field.

The two authors of this volume symbolise the strategic positioning of MEMOS: the link between theory and practice. They are from the worlds of academia and fieldwork, worlds that exist side by side but often do so without communicating. They also have backgrounds in the world of sport. For many years, Alain Ferrand has been teaching sport management at the Claude Bernard University in Lyon, France, after having studied physical education, economics, and psychology. Luiggino Torrigiani is the head of a management consulting firm in Lausanne, Switzerland, after having been the marketing director of two International Sports Federations based in the Olympic capital. Alain and Luiggino met thanks to MEMOS and since have been collaborating closely every year teaching the module devoted to marketing management. They form a team of which the likes are rare and in which each complements and learns from the other.

My wish is for this work to have as much success as their partnership and for readers to share their dedicated enthusiasm and their many competencies regarding this subject that is essential for the future of the Olympic sports organisations.

Professor Jean-Loup Chappelet,
MEMOS Director

* MEMOS network academic members in 2005

Ecole nationale d'éducation physique et des sports de Luxembourg, Luxemburg

Institut de hautes études en administration publique, Lausanne, Switzerland

Institut Nacional d'Educacio Fisica de Catalunya, Lleida and Barcelona, Spain

Institut national du sport et de l'éducation physique, Paris, France

Loughborough University (Institute of Sport and Leisure Policy), Loughborough, United Kingdom

Scuola dello Sport dello Comitato Olimpico Nazionale Italiano, Roma, Italy

Université Claude Bernard Lyon 1 (Faculté des sciences du sport), Lyon, France

Università degli studi di San Marino (Dipartimento di Economia e Tecnologia), San Marino

Université Libre de Bruxelles (Solvay Businesss School and ISEPK), Bruxelles, Belgium

Universidade Lusófona de Humanidades e Tecnologias, Lisboa, Portugal

Acknowledgments

This book is the result of a friendship and the matching of two complementary experiences within MEMOS. Furthermore, its contents are enriched with the participants' expertise working on five continents. We wish to send special thanks to two of them, Filippo Bazzanella (Marcialonga CEO) and Damjan Pintar (Slovenian Olympic Committee Marketing Director), for their direct collaboration on this book.

Introduction

In the first volume, titled Strategic and Performance Management of Olympic Sport Organisations, Chappelet and Bayle (2004) define Olympic sport organisations (OSOs) as "organisations that belong to the Olympic system and to the sports movement: clubs, National Sport Federations, International Federations, National Olympic Committees, Organising Committees, etc.". We notice two opposite trends. Those organisations that are making a profit in order to use it to further the activities they organise, for example professional soccer clubs, appear to want to focus on seeking the values that once reigned only over social organisations, such as the welfare of the individual within society. Inversely, the "social" sport organisations are more and more concerned with the economic effectiveness of their activity. However, by rationalising their management, they wish to preserve a participative culture.

A marketing approach is more and more legitimate in sport organisations. However, the meaning of this term can be misunderstood, particularly because a large number of definitions exist. Of course, each author attempts to bring his or her personal touch. Baumann (2000) proposes a simple, operational definition—marketing is the "operational implementation of its instruments, which creates guidelines for managing the products and services. Its vocation is to respond to the needs of the potential consumers/buyers in order to guarantee the success of the enterprise in the form of profits". In this context, we consider that marketing is a process based on the notion of the mutually satisfactory exchange between a sport organisation and its users. Whatever its size and its sphere of influence, an OSO must satisfy its members and inspire their loyalty. It must develop in comparison to the competition and find resources for itself (financial, human, etc.) in order to be able to achieve the objectives that it has set for itself. For an OSO, the marketing approach makes it possible to take into account the political, economic, institutional, technological, and cultural environment in order to determine, with precision, the target groups (members, users, and consumers) it wishes to address. It also enables the organisation to study the tangible and intangible expectations of these groups in order to offer them the products and services that are the most appropriate to satisfy them or to lead them to change their behaviour.

The Specific Character of OSO Marketing

Olympic sport organisation marketing has a specific character. The association defends a cause, and its marketing goes beyond the immediate demand that is mainly linked to seeking financial profit. It works towards improving life within society and thus contributes towards changing it. An athletics club does not simply exchange a service (training, organising competitions, etc.) for money (subscription fees). It carries out a social transaction within which its action procures benefits for its members. These benefits are linked to a project for societal development aiming to enable those practising the sport to enjoy a better life.

An OSO is committed to a social and cultural project. It will therefore not change this project in order to adopt a different, more fashionable one. It can orient its marketing around five areas, presented in table 0.1.

The strategy relating to marketing thus consists of different orientations or dimensions. It develops by taking into account two types of factors. On an internal level, such factors as history, the mission, and the objectives must be taken into account. On an external level, competitors, cultural and economic tendencies, and so on must be borne in mind. Marketing is situated within a process that is integrated within the sport organisation's strategy.

What Is Understood By or Perceived As Marketing in Sport Organisations

Marketing is not a question of method alone. Creating and developing a marketing function in sport organisations is influenced by what the term marketing is seen to mean, on the one hand, and by the operational problems it is supposed to resolve on the other. When those managing a sport organisation are asked what they associate with the word 'marketing', in fact, a great many responses are obtained, including the following:

- Sponsoring
- Publicity
- Spending without certainty of profitability
- That's for the executive committee to do
- It's the key to success
- It creates a good image
- Using the "marketing mix"

Table 0.1 The Five Areas of Sport Organisation Marketing

Area	Objectives	Target groups
Project pursued by the OSO: → Internal marketing	• Conveying the information • Developing membership loyalty • Motivating volunteers and staff	• Members • Volunteers • Paid staff • Board of directors
The OSO itself: → Corporate marketing	• Managing its brand equity • Raising funds • Developing its influence • Lobbying	• Mass public • Users • Those in authority • Opinion leaders
Search for private financing: → Fund-raising marketing	• Developing sponsorship and fund-raising	• Companies • Public and private institutions
Services offered: → Services marketing	• Improving the quality of service in order to satisfy target expectations • Providing incitement to join the OSO	• Members (defensive strategy) • Potential members (offensive strategy)
Incitement or prevention: → Social cause marketing	• Convincing target audience of sport practice benefits: health, personal development, social integration, and so on	• Mass public • Public concerned

Analysing the operational dimensions, which corresponds to implementing the strategy drawn up for achieving an objective on the terrain involved, makes it possible to identify the needs regarding marketing.

1. For companies, sport sponsoring is an interesting vector for communication because it enables the company to show the effectiveness of products, to promote values, and so on.

2. The communication objective is to increase the organisation's media presence.

3. Promoting the services of the sport organisation attracts members to join.

4. Analysing the market compared with the organisational mission and the competition helps the company to define a coherent strategy.

These representations are set forth in table 0.2.

Prior to being a set of tools and methods, marketing corresponds to a vision, to a perception, and to a philosophy of the market. It helps the sport organisation succeed in its mission. It is, of course, a perception that is anchored both in the organisation's history and in the way it sees

the operational questions that it must resolve in order to take action in its market.

Operating in an Increasingly Open and Competitive Area

Each OSO can be situated in an area defined by two axes. The first axis concerns its relation with its environment. The organisation can remain closed in on itself. In this case, it communicates little with its environment, and the changes that take place in this environment have little effect on it. In the opposite case, that is, in an open structure, the organisation will seek to adapt itself to the environment and to the existing competition. The other axis concerns the mode of sociability and its objectives. Individuals who are in a "convivial" system favour interpersonal relations based on affinities. For the organisation, the purpose is above all to establish a good climate by ensuring that people get along well together. A rational system becomes organised, specialised, and formalised in order to become more effective regarding its self-appointed objectives (see figure 0.1).

It is becoming increasingly difficult for large organisations such as the national and international sport federations to develop while

Table 0.2 The Perceptions of Marketing in Sport Organisations

Phase	Objectives for the sport organisation	Competitive advantages
Focus: sponsoring	Finding financial partners	Sport makes it possible to reveal the effectiveness of products, to promote values.
Focus: media coverage	Increasing the presence of sport and events in the media (notably television) in order to promote the sport and make it more attractive for the sponsors	Sport is a cultural phenomenon that involves an increasing number of people.
Focus: market	Increasing the number of members	Individuals exist who have not been actively prospected and who could practice the sports and become members of the sport organisations.
Focus: demand	Analysing and managing all relations linking the consumers, the product, the competition, and the sport organisation in order to create a competitive advantage and to establish positioning	Here, this means taking into account the expectations of individuals in a way that satisfies them more than offers by the competition.

remaining in a convivial/closed configuration. The marketing approach contributes towards rationalising the organisation's approach, from both an internal and an external point of view. This approach is not neutral, however, and provokes tensions within the organisation that take the form of a dilemma whose elements are presented in figure 0.2.

The organisation becomes a place where services corresponding to the expectations of its members are provided, within a competitive context. In order to provide a satisfactory service, the structure develops professional services (including those related to market-

ing), and it must face up to an ever-increasing pressure linked to the quality of services. This situation incites us to interrelate professional competencies, notably in the area of marketing and the organisation's situation.

Finding a Balance Between Societal and Economic Profitability

Marketing is thus not a universal approach. There are, however, several conceptions of marketing that portray the same state of mind, as defined by Vernette (1998): "Marketing is the methodical, ongoing conquest of a profitable market, implying the conception and commercialisation of a product or service that is in line with the expectations of the consumers targeted". All marketing definitions refer to clients, consumers, and profit and are not in line with the approach of OSOs. Chappelet (2004) stressed that OSOs as "non-profit organisations have members and stakeholders rather than customers and clients; they depend on many volunteers; they have usually a two-level governance made up of elected officials and hired managers; they also are more open to public opinion scrutiny ("Publicness") than the for-profit commercial companies". Figure 0.3 presents International Olympic Committee stakeholders, organised according to two axes: their situation (internal or external) and the length of their relationship (medium term or long term). Nevertheless, depending on the

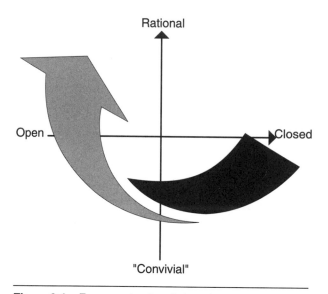

Figure 0.1 From a natural and closed sector to a rational and open one.

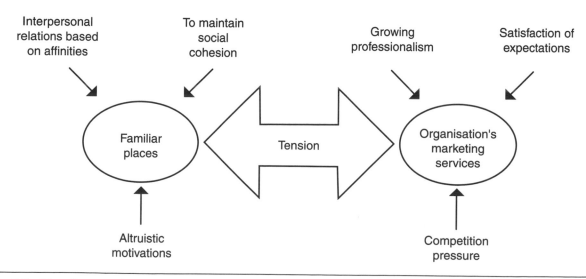

Figure 0.2 The dilemma of sport organisations seeking to open up to their environment.

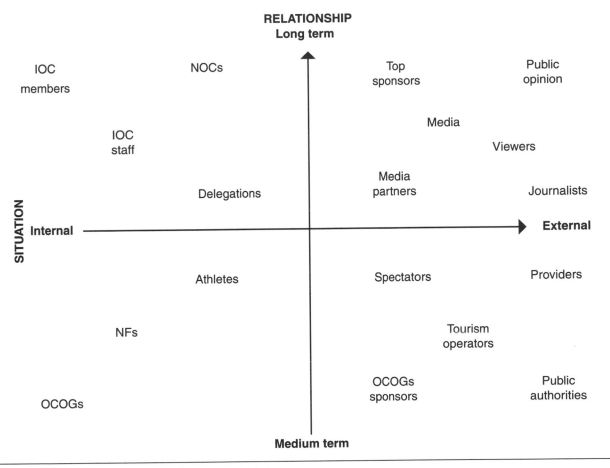

Figure 0.3 International Olympic Committee stakeholders.

situation, we will use the generic terms: clients, consumers, partners, members, and stakeholders. They all have different expectations, and marketing helps an OSO to develop services aimed at satisfying them. These services must be consistent with its mission.

Furthermore, profitability can be defined on the basis of economic criteria and of those related to the mission. An OSO exists in relation to the mission as stated in its statutes. Generally speaking, this mission is to promote the practice of a specific sport in all its forms, while permitting individuals to live a better life within society. An OSO develops societal marketing that aims to improve the well-being of consumers and of society. Economic profitability must also be assured. An OSO exists within an economic system with income (subscriptions, sponsors, subsidies, etc.) and expenditure that must be balanced. We thus gain a better grasp of the term "profitable market". This is illustrated by the objectives of "Olympic marketing":

- "To ensure the future of sport by contributing to Olympic athletes from every nation and by providing for the staging of the Olympic Games

- To preserve the special character of the Olympic Games, to protect and promote the Olympic image and ideals throughout the world, and to work with all marketing partners to enhance Olympism

- To create continuing long-term marketing programmes and to build on and support the successful activities developed by each Organising Committee, thus ensuring the financial stability of the Olympic Movement

- To ensure appropriate distribution of revenue throughout the Olympic Movement, including future Organising Committees, National Olympic Committees, International Federations and other recognised organisations

- To ensure that the whole world can view and experience the Olympic Games via free-to-air television" (IOC[1])

Focus and Structure of the Book

This book is addressed to managers from OSOs, their stakeholders, and the organisations in relation to this system. All of these have to deal with issues linked to strategic or to operational marketing. We develop these concepts in this book. Strategic marketing analyses the resources and competences in relation to the environment in which the organisation evolves in order to react to threats (economic, legislative, competition, etc.) and to benefit from opportunities. Operational marketing testifies to a voluntarist approach. It aims at exploiting in the short run existing opportunities of the market.

Within the framework of this book we privilege the strategic approach, taking into account the fact that it directs OSO action and that it engages its resources in a medium- or long-term perspective. Furthermore, it is a critical issue that allows an adaptation of the organisation in its environment. In this context, we have retained four critical topics that an OSO has to master. Each is developed in a specific chapter, illustrated by a case study.

The first chapter focuses on OSO brand equity management. Each organisation possesses a brand, which is a source of value both for the OSO and for its stakeholders. We present a framework aiming at assessing and managing assets, for example awareness, image, perceived quality, loyalty, and protection. This chapter presents the Marcialonga—the largest Italian cross-country ski race and a part of the Worldloppet.

The second chapter provides tools and methods in order to analyse stakeholders' expectations and their decision-making processes. This will allow OSO marketers to better understand these stakeholder characteristics. Stakeholders are both rational and emotional. Nevertheless, in a sport area they are looking for an emotional experience. We illustrate this experiential marketing approach with the FIVB Beach Volleyball World Tour.

The third chapter tackles the strategic marketing issue. Strategy is an ongoing process aimed at getting into an attractive position in your marketplace and developing resources and competences that are superior to those of the competitors. An offering will not build values unless these two requirements are simultaneously met. This analysis is illustrated by the case of a French professional soccer club: Olympique Lyonnais.

The fourth chapter relates to strategic sponsorship management. This chapter enabled us to specify the sponsoring persuasive impact in order to develop a model that makes it possible to work out strategic choices relating to sponsorship. This sensitive topic is developed with the Slovenian Olympic Committee.

---

[1] www.olympic.org

Developing the Olympic Sport Organisation's Brand Equity

The title of this chapter may appear surprising, given the association of the terms "Olympic sport organisation" and "brand". This seems to be an indicator that business marketing developed by organisations is moving towards lucrative commercial activity. Every sport organisation possesses a brand, and our aim is to show that it is in the interests of all sport organisations to develop their brand equity through a marketing approach. First, we define the concept of a brand, and then we show that a brand is valuable for both the sport organisation and its members and partners. Finally, we deal with the evaluation and management of the brand's assets.

Within the framework of this chapter, we develop in particular the case of Marcialonga.[1] This is the biggest Italian country ski race. It is one of 14 Worldloppet[2] events throughout the world.

EXHIBIT 1.1 MARCIALONGA: ONE YEAR FOR ONE DAY

The idea of the Marcialonga goes back a long way, the result of the fascination exerted for years by the Swedish Vasaloppet, the undisputed leader in the field of international cross-country skiing competitions. The four founders wanted to create something similar, adding typically Italian warmth and enthusiasm, seasoned with lots of imagination, to the challenge of covering such long distances (70 km).

On February 7, 1971, the Fiemme and Fassa valleys heard the echo of the cannon shot, which signalled the start of the first Marcialonga, destined to revolutionise the history and traditions of skiing enthusiasts.

It is the track that forms the most important part of Marcialonga. Metre after metre, it measures out the heart of a mountain landscape, with its unequalled qualities and great traditions. Through the Marcialonga, the Fiemme and Fassa valleys open up their history, culture, and traditions to the world, revealing people who are reserved but who maintain their true identity in this rapidly changing world.

Competing in the Marcialonga and skiing through the villages, athletes breathe in the charm of a world that brims with real values, and the genuineness of people who are still refreshingly spontaneous.

For more than 30 years, Marcialonga has been an extraordinary event in human and emotional terms, creating friendship and entertainment. It attracts hundreds of volunteers working together, motivated solely by the appeal of the competition. Mass participation beyond comparison is shown continuously throughout the event, whether in technical assistance or competitiveness or in

---

[1] www.marcialonga.it/

[2] Worldloppet Ski Federation (Worldloppet) is an international sport federation of cross-country skiing marathons. The federation was founded in 1978 in Uppsala, Sweden. The aim of Worldloppet is to promote the sport of cross-country skiing through various ski races around the world. www.worldloppet.com

terms of a great welcome. Over 150,000 participants have taken part in Marcialonga over a period
of 30 years. Of these, only 65,000 are Italian, and
85,000 are foreign skiers coming from more than
30 nations from all over the world. These figures
clearly illustrate the importance of Marcialonga at
an international level.

Filippo Bazzanella, Marcialonga CEO

1.1 What Is a Brand?

The American Marketing Association (AMA)
defines a brand as "a name, term, design,
symbol, or any other feature that identifies one
seller's good or service as distinct from those
of other sellers". Usually brands are registered
(trademarked) with a regulatory authority and
so cannot be used freely by other parties. Lehu
(1996) develops these two dimensions: "A brand
is a semantic factor of distinctive designation
of products offered on a market by a producer
or a distributor. It can be a name of one or more
words, geographical or otherwise, a patronym, a
pseudonym, a name used as an acronym or in the
form of an abbreviation, to which can be associated a symbol, a colour, a font and a character
size. A genuine right to ownership, a precious
asset that a company must constantly capitalise
upon, the brand plays a strategic role and can be
the subject of a transfer of ownership or an agreement concerning user rights under licence".

From the point of view of Marcialonga, which
constitutes our reference brand, this definition
permits us to specify its features in table 1.1.

It is acknowledged and emphasised that the
majority of sporting organisations do not wish
or are not able to sell their brand; this is subject

to the rules of commercial rights. The legal term
for a brand is a trademark. "A brand may identify one item, a family of items, or all items of
that seller. If used for the firm as a whole, the
preferred term is trade name" (AMA).

The Brand As a Source of Value for the Organisation and Its Stakeholders

This approach to the brand remains descriptive.
The dynamic approach to the brand takes into
account its value for both the organisation and
the consumer. We have stressed the importance
of loyalty: Kapferer and Laurent (1993) revealed
that consumers were, to varying degrees, sensitive to the brand and that brands were taken into
account in cases of perceived risk (of making the
wrong choice in terms of financial or security
aspects, etc.). A brand is reassuring when it
offers a guarantee of quality and security. People
prefer, for instance, to call upon the Mountain
Guide Company in Chamonix if they are not
able to handle high-altitude mountaineering
alone. In the area of sport, sensitivity to a brand
is measured for professional teams. Spectators
do not go to see a football match, but to see
"their" team. This fact reveals the relation that
exists between the club and its supporters.

Kapferer (1998) draws up an exhaustive list of
the functions of brands for consumers. Analysis
shows that Marcialonga participant interview
content is in line with eight functions.

1. Situating: For example, "Marcialonga is
a international cross-country ski race organised
in the Fassa and Fiemme valleys (Italy)" provides a clear view to participants and situates
the offer in a product category.

2. Practicality: For example, "Every year I
am not bothering about the race I want to be part
of: It is Marcialonga. Skiers are saving time and
energy".

3. Guarantee: "Marcialonga is a well-
organised event by competent people". Participants are sure of finding a stable quality
everywhere, whatever the place and time.

4. Optimisation: "Marcialonga is the best
cross-country marathon race in Italy". Participants
are sure of buying the best product in the category,
the best performance for this specific use.

5. Personalisation: "I consider that participating to Marcialonga is expressing my person-

Table 1.1 Marcialonga Features

Characteristics	Marcialonga
Brand is a distinctive sign	MARCIALONGA
Mission, activity	• Cross-country ski racing • Italy and world • Unique experience through Fiemme and Fassa valleys in Trentino
Brand owners	• Marcialonga S.c.a.r.l. • Ski Club Marcialonga (non-profit-making organisation)

Marcialonga logo courtesy of MARCIALONGA S.C.A.R.L.

ality". The Marcialonga brand is in line with skiers' self-image as projected to others.

6. Permanence: "This is the third time I am participating in Marcialonga and I am promoting this event among my friends". This testifies to satisfaction born of the familiarity and intimacy of links to Marcialonga.

7. Hedonism: "I am rather satisfied to be part of Marcialonga because of the friendly atmosphere, the scenery, and the authenticity of the race". Pleasure is related to satisfaction linked to the brand's experience, aesthetics, design, and communications.

8. Ethics: "Marcialonga organisation does care about ecology and sport ethics". Participant satisfaction is related to the responsible behaviour of the brand in its relationship with society.

Although not all functions are equally useful to a sport organisation, it remains true that the consumer benefits mentioned express the existence of a relation between the brand and the people who use it. The importance of these benefits and the brand's capacity to satisfy them express the value of the brand for the consumer.

This essential point leads us to define the brand as an entity that possesses a relation with the sport organisation's stakeholders. Stakeholders are those who have an interest in a particular decision, either as individuals or as representatives of a group. This includes people who influence a decision, or *can* influence it, as well as those affected by it. Freeman's (1984) seminal conception was that stakeholders included all affecters and affectees of corporate policies and activities (i.e., all relevant interests). The distinction means that stakeholdership implies the union of influence (i.e., affecters) and impact (i.e., affectees). Depending on its position (sport governing body vs. club) and its geographical area (international vs. national), an OSO has various kinds of stakeholders: staff, members, clubs, national federations, media, sponsors, government, and so on. This relation is defined by the type of benefits the brand is providing to the stakeholder (functional, symbolic, sociocultural, emotional) and their influence on the OSO's decisions or impact on them. Chappelet (2004) analyses the new "Olympic system" as presented in figure 1.1.

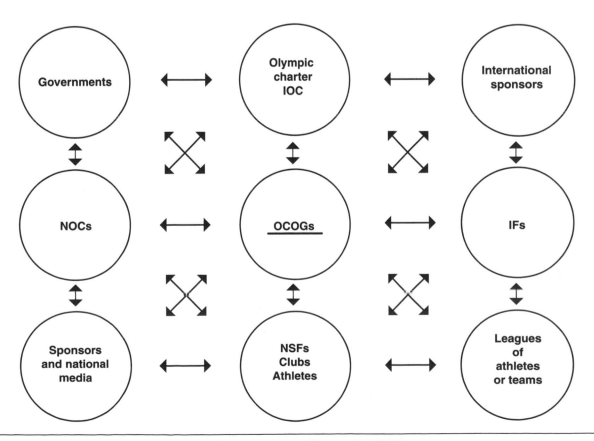

Figure 1.1 The new actors encircling the Olympic system (Chappelet, 2004).

The Brand As a Source of Value for the Sport Organisation

The brand falls within a logic of differentiated offering. According to Kapferer (1998), the organisation wishes to better satisfy the expectations of a segment of the clientele by supplying it, in a "constant and repeated way, with the ideal combination of tangible and intangible, functional and hedonistic attributes . . . in conditions that are economically viable for it". The sport organisation thus marks its sector by putting its stamp on the product. When thinking of athletics in Italy, for example, we think of FIDAL (Federazione Italiana di Atletica Leggera).[3] For the federation, this means

- associating the benefits linked to the practice of athletics in clubs,
- associating the factors of the services, and
- demonstrating competitive advantages in comparison with other sports (direct competition) and with a nonstructured personal type of practice (running).

Earlier we saw that sport is in a competitive situation when the question is one of satisfying motives such as relaxing and making friends. Certain sport organisations find themselves in direct competition with commercial structures that propose similar sport services, or within the context of sponsoring for events. Moreover, the brand permits the sport organisation to create sponsorship opportunities for itself. We shall devote chapter 4 to this area, whose strategic importance is increasing. Sponsoring also opens up possibilities for brand extensions. This is the case of merchandising for a sport organisation and the events it controls. Some of these can give rise to licensing contracts.

Sport Organisation Brand Equity

Today's understanding of brand takes it far beyond the AMA definition. Brand is now more commonly defined as a set of expectations and associations evoked from experience with a sport organisation or a service that it provides (e.g., an event). It's all about how stakeholders think and feel about what the organisation and its services actually deliver across the board. If the expectations, associations, and experiences are positive, negative, and neutral, these combine to create the brand's equity. Brand equity has been conceptualised in a variety of ways. Cooper and Simons (1997) consider brand equity as the strength, currency, and value of the brand; the description, and assessment of the appeal, of a brand to all target audiences who interact with it. As noted authority David Aaker (1991) defines brand equity; it is the set of assets and liabilities that connects "a brand to its name or its symbols and that brings something to the enterprise and to its clients because they give an added value or a lesser value to the products and to the services". The assets and the liability that the brand entity includes must be linked to the brand's name, its symbols (logo, packaging, etc.), or both. If the name or logo is changed, all or part of these assets are perturbed or even lost even if certain factors can be transferred to the brand's new name or its new visual symbols. As Aaker detailed in his classic *Managing Brand Equity*, creating a brand equity profile involves the identification of the various customer associations with a brand, as well as levels of customer awareness and loyalty that set it apart from competitors.

According to this definition, brand equity is created in the mind of consumers in the marketplace (taking into account the competitors). It can add to or remove value from an OSO service or product. Kohli and Leuthesser (2001) synthesised these two aspects: Brand equity is defined as "the differential effect of brand knowledge on customer response". Three elements of this definition need to be emphasised.

- Differential (e.g., differentiation) is the most critical, because a brand must be perceived as different from the others (competitors).
- Brand knowledge—your customers should know about the differentiation and should appreciate that the differentiation is meaningful for them.
- Customer response—customers should respond favourably to this differentiation, for example with loyalty or with

---

[3] www.fidal.it

willingness to pay a premium for their preference.

1.2 Measuring Brand Equity

Over the past decade, mainstream marketing studies have focused significant attention on the assessment and measurement of brand equity (see table 1.2) and the use of brand equity in brand extensions, but little research has been conducted on assessing sport organisation brand equity (Gladden, Milne, and Sutton [1998]; Gladden and Milne [1999]; Ross [2002]; Ross and James [2003]).

The asset and liability factors of the brand equity are varied and differ according to the cases in question. However, they refer to OSO stakeholders and can be broken down into six main categories (figure 1.2):

1. Foundations
2. Legal protection
3. Knowledge
4. Experience
5. Relationship
6. Stakeholders

Olympic Sport Organisation Brand Foundations

The foundations are the bases of your brand. You must be consistent with its history and its vision in order to define its identity.

Brand Heritage

Any OSO brand is related to its history, and it inherits any attributes, immaterial characteristics, and practices that are handed down from the past by tradition. From a corporate perspective a brand's heritage is the experience and the reputation that a brand has acquired over time, including its origins and communication development (Abimbola, Saunders, and Broderick, 1999). A brand has to be consistent with its history even if the history is a short one. Ask yourself: What is the heritage of this brand, and do I fully understand it?

Table 1.2 Different Approaches to Measuring Brand Equity

Authors	Dimensions assessed
D.A. Aaker, 1991	• Awareness • Brand associations (e.g., image) • Perceived quality • Loyalty • Other assets (e.g., competitive advantage, registered trademark, relationship with distribution networks)
J.N. Kapferer, 1998	• Awareness • Perceived quality related to competition • Level of confidence, pertinence, empathy and esteem • Brand's imaginary richness and attractiveness • Immaterial values in relation with brand consumption
Interbrand, 2003	• Market (10%)—this is the structural attractiveness of the market, its projected growth • Stability (15%)—brands that have been established for a long time that constantly command customer loyalty • Leadership (25%)—the ability of the brand to influence the market • Trend (10%)—the brand's ability to remain contemporary and relevant to consumers • Support (10%)—the quantity and quality of investments made to support the brand • Internationalisation/Geography (25%)—the brand's attractiveness and appeal in a multiplicity of markets with a view to distinguish between regional, national and international brands • Protection (5%)—the protection received from the legal system, patents, and trademarks

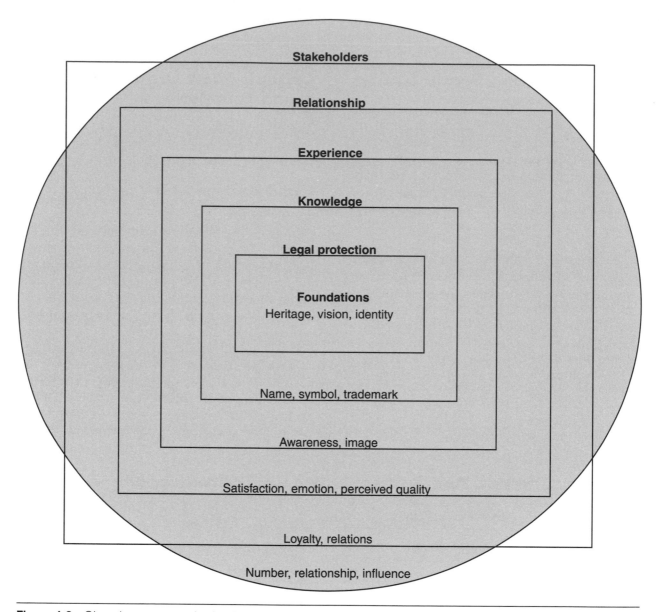

Figure 1.2 Olympic sport organisation brand equity dimensions.

EXHIBIT 1.2 THE MARCIALONGA HERITAGE

In 1969, four Italian men officially took part in the Vasaloppet for the first time; 1970 saw a repeat, with about 30 people taking part, including the first four men. As enthusiasm mounted, there arose the idea of creating something similar, adding typically Italian warmth and enthusiasm, seasoned with lots of imagination, to the exertion of covering such long distances.

The first problem was where to hold an event of this size, and the two valleys of Fiemme and Fassa immediately came to mind, an area where Franco Nones, the first Italian cross-country skiing winner

of an Olympic gold medal (30 km men's in Grenoble 1968), is living. Here in the Italian cradle of cross-country skiing were two mountain schools, one for the customs service and one for the police; they provided men and means. This was a good basis from the organisational point of view, while the task of creating the image, perhaps even more difficult, was entrusted to the zeal and competence of the first secretary general, Mr. Roberto Moggio. This delicate task entailed going from village to village, where traditional parochialism was soon put aside in the desire to work together towards a single goal. The first edition was to be held in 1971, the year in which the FISI (Italian Winter Sports Federations) celebrated its 50th anniversary.

But what should the event be called? Open to everyone, the event was becoming better known, and 50,000 leaflets were dropped from an aeroplane over the valleys of Fiemme and Fassa to promote it among the inhabitants. In the end the name "Marcialonga" (or Long March) was chosen as it was felt to neatly encapsulate the idea of the hard work and friendly competition of the athletes as well as the involvement of the spectators before such great entertainment. When the votes were counted, there was a surprise: The originator of the idea was Roberto Moggio himself, who not only had a decisive personal touch at this early stage but also was full of exciting ideas.

Filippo Bazzanella, Marcialonga CEO

Brand Vision

Olympic sport organisation vision provides an answer to the following question: Where do we want to be? This is an important aspect of strategic management. According to Chappelet (2004), a "vision refers to shared values that are implied and to an ideal that is difficult to attain and as such, often not expressed". An OSO's brand vision must be consistent with its overall vision. To this end the brand values have to be clearly specified (table 1.3). The term "value" has been defined as an enduring prescriptive or proscriptive belief that a specific end state of existence or specific mode of conduct is preferred to an opposite end state or mode of conduct for living one's life (Kahle, 1983; Rokeach, 1973; Schwartz, 1992). This refers to personal values, and these can be extended to OSO brand values.

Two organisations control the Marcialonga brand. Marcialonga S.c.a.r.l. and Ski Club Marcialonga have specific values and common values as presented in figure 1.3.

Brand Identity

Brand identity "is a unique set of brand associations that the brand strategist aspires to create or maintain. These associations represent what the brand stands for and imply a promise to customers by the organisation" (Aaker, 1996).

Table 1.3 **List of Brand Values**

What are the fundamental beliefs and values that drive the OSO brand?	
Community	Ecology
Nurturing	Health
Innovation	Responsiveness
Tradition	Education
Diversity	Pragmatism
Reliability	Sense of urgency
Trust	People
Positive outlook	Precision
Irreverence	Safety
Overdelivery	Affordability
Teamwork	Integrity
Family	Knowledge
Competitiveness	Quality
Entertainment	Cleanliness
Connection	Fairness
Authenticity	Security
Commitment	Honesty
Disclosure	Heritage
Fun	Growth
Performance	Customer focus
Simplicity	Creativity
Competence	Responsibility
Noncompetitive spirit	Entrepreneurship

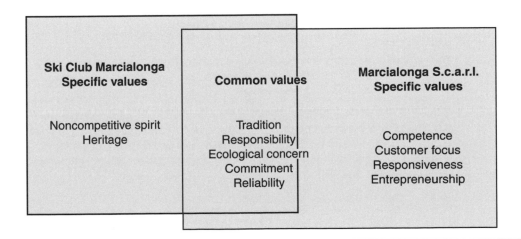

Figure 1.3 Marcialonga governing bodies' values.

According to this author, brand identity aims at creating and developing a relationship with the brand, generating a value proposition based on functional, emotional or self-expressive benefits. Kapferer (1998) stressed that the identity concept is crucial because a brand needs to be durable, to send out coherent signs, and to be realistic. In this way the identity must take on and count as the brand image. The stakeholders tie this up in the perception of the brand.

If brand image refers to the current perception of the brand, brand identity specifies how strategists want the brand to be perceived. Identity is on the OSO side. The purpose is to specify the brand's meaning. Before projecting an image to the public, we must know exactly what we want to project. Aaker (1996) stressed four dimensions in order to specify the brand identity (table 1.4):

- Brand as a product: product scope, product attributes, quality, value, use, users, and country of origin
- Brand as organisation: organisation attributes (e.g., innovation, consumer concern, trustworthiness), local versus global
- Brand as a person: personality (e.g., genuine, energetic, rugged)
- Brand as a symbol: visual imagery and metaphors

The part of the brand identity and value proposition actively communicated to an OSO target audience specifies the brand position.

The Marcialonga logo is appreciated by the three target groups—participants, spectators, and distant spectators (via the Internet). Figure 1.4 presents the results of a survey conducted by questionnaire.

Legal Protection

Can you put your organisation in a position to protect the investment that you're going to put into the brand? Are you going to put at risk your sponsorship and licensing rights? Or, what can you do to stop your competitors from ripping off the look, the sound, the colour, the theme, or the language of your branding strategy? Broadly speaking, you get rights to your brand, that is, the power to use the law to stop someone else from getting too close to it. One of the main legal ways of protecting a brand is through a trademark registration. But not everything you might think of using as a brand can be registered as a trademark.

Legal Definition of Brand

A trademark or a mark[4] is a word, a name, a symbol, a device, or a combination of these that indicates the source of goods or services. It distin-

Table 1.4 Marcialonga Brand Identity

Dimensions	Characteristics
Marcialonga as a product	• A world cross-country ski race—part of Worldloppet • The best Italian race • Track passing through the villages in Fassa and Fiemme valleys • Users: top athletes and anyone who wants to have an authentic experience • Motives: to compete, participate, enjoy, experience the pleasure of completing the race, meet friends and other people, etc.
Marcialonga as an organisation	• Competent, reliable, and responsive • Professionals and volunteers • Local and international
Marcialonga as a person	• Marcialonga is endorsed by participants (world-class competitors associated with the "bisons", e.g., the crowd of amateur skiers) and volunteers • Warmth, communicativeness, and sense of achievement • Community member, intending to preserve and enhance the welfare of people
Brand as a symbol	• Marcialonga logo, which is appreciated

[4]A service mark is used in connection with services, while a trademark is used in connection with tangible goods. The general terms "mark" or "trademark" may be used to describe both trademarks and service marks.

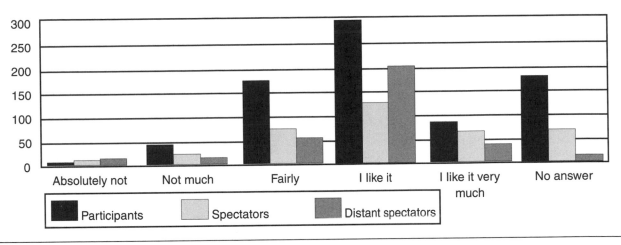

Figure 1.4 Appreciation of Marcialonga logo.

Reprinted, by permission, from Bazzanella, P. 2003. Developing sport event brand equity: The Marcialonga case. MEMOS dissertation. Université Claude Bernard, Lyon.

guishes the products or services of one business from those of others in the same field. Trademark definitions can vary a little from one country to another. Nevertheless, the primary rule of registration is that the sign must be distinctive (this can be tested using consumer awareness). Distinctiveness includes words, designs, letters, numerals, shape of goods (3D), packaging shapes (3D), sounds, smells, and colours (only some particular colours in specific contexts).

Trademark ownership must be claimed and expressed to competitors by the use of the following symbols:

TM—indicates that the work is a trademark but that it is unregistered[5] (FIFA World Cup™)

®—signifies that the trademark or service mark has been registered with the relevant trademark registry (Marcialonga®)

European and U.S. Features

Registering a trademark means going through formal procedures, which result in your trademark's being officially recorded as belonging to your business. Registration gives you the exclusive right to use that mark and to sue someone else who uses that same mark or something similar to it on the same products or similar products.

The registration of your trademark by the appropriate authority in one country does not protect you in another country. The classic method consists of depositing the trademark with the national office of each of the countries in which you wish to protect it. This approach operates within an international framework.

The Madrid Agreement The Madrid Agreement allows a trademark registered in one country to be registered in other countries and territories. The Madrid system comprises two treaties: the Madrid Agreement Concerning the International Registration of Marks, which dates from 1891, and the Protocol Relating to the Madrid Agreement, which came into operation on April 1, 1996. The full name of the system of treaties is "Madrid Agreement Concerning the International Registration of Marks of April 14, 1891 (as revised at Brussels on December 14, 1900, at Washington on June 2, 1911, at The Hague on November 6, 1925, at London on June 2, 1934, at Nice on June 15, 1957, and at Stockholm on July 14, 1967)".

The Madrid Agreement provides for international registration of trademarks. This is very useful for trademark owners who engage in international trade and wish to gain protection in other countries for their brand, or who have built up a reputation in a mark that transcends borders and want to protect intellectual property pirates from appropriating their mark.

The request is transmitted via the national office to the international office of the OMPI (World Organisation of Intellectual Property).

---

[5] The 2002 FIFA World Cup Rights Protection Programme. FIFA is the world governing body of association football and controls the FIFA World Cup.

The international request specifies the countries in which protection is requested. It includes a reproduction of the mark, as well as the list of products and services for which the mark is registered. If the registration is accepted, the trademark is incorporated into the international register. The protection is effective for the duration of 10 years and can be extended.

The agreement originally intended to provide for an international registration system, but did not achieve this due to a lack of international acceptance. Many nonmember countries including the United Kingdom, the United States, and Central American, South American, and Asian countries such as Japan were not adherents, which undermined recognition of the system as a truly "international" regime. Significantly, many of these countries are among the world's foremost sources of trademark registrations.

European Community Trade Mark   The European Community Trade Mark (ECTM) system, created in 1996, is open to countries outside of the EC. The community mark is a unique title, obtained by a unique procedure and valid in all the territories of the EC. The Office for Harmonization in the Internal Market (OHIM) examines and registers the community trademarks, allowing protection at the best cost.

U.S. Trademark Law   The Lanham Act (1946, revised in 1988) is similar to the laws of other countries. In 1994 the United States signed the Trade Mark Treaty, intended to harmonise global trademark legislation.

Despite these attempts at harmonisation, there is little cross-border protection. Consequently it is vital to register a trademark in every strategic country. This needs to be done by a professional who has the expertise to search and check databases and manage any legal issues.

The selection of countries where the trademark must be protected is a strategic choice. This choice takes into account the market in which the OSO operates, local legislation, and possibilities of defending its rights. Thus, it is fairly difficult to put in place a working uniform strategy for all countries.

Trademark Application Procedure

The procedure for registration is different for each country, but the following list provides an outline of the usual process required (Ellwood, 2000).

- Selection and definition of the precise trademark (and its class[6])
- Search of trademark databases to ensure that the mark is unique and not likely to be rejected
- Application for registration (one to several countries)
- Trademark registration and publication (there is a period of several months during which anyone can file an objection)
- Issuance of a registration certificate

Likelihood of Confusion

The principle of likelihood of confusion in the mind of the consumer is the basis of most court judgements. Kohli and Thakor (1997) have indicated that the likelihood of confusion can be broken down into seven categories:

- Degree of similarity between the marks in appearance and suggestion
- The similarity of the products
- The area and the manner of use
- The degree of care likely to be exercised
- The strength of the plaintiff's remarks
- Actual confusion
- Intent of the alleged infringer

Marcialonga Trademark

The Marcialonga is a European Community Trade Mark registered in October 2001 (20 years after the first edition). It refers to two categories: events and clothes. In 2003 the Marcialonga Magazine brand was registered as a European Community Trade Mark for press publishing. The Marcialonga logo design is shown here. Marcialonga S.c.a.r.l. is the brand owner. Ski Club Marcialonga is the event owner. The same group of persons manages these two organisations.

Courtesy of MARCIALONGA S.C.A.R.L.

---

[6] There are 45 international trademark classes: 34 for goods and 11 for services.

Knowledge

As soon as you act and communicate, your brand is going to be fixed in people's minds. The first stage of knowledge concerns awareness, and the second relates to image.

Brand Awareness

For an organisation, awareness corresponds to being known within a given population. In the strict sense, awareness corresponds to being recognised or referred to.

Prompted and Unprompted Awareness There are two types of awareness that are strongly correlated. Prompt awareness corresponds to the percentage of individuals capable of citing the name of the sport organisation spontaneously within the universe of the given service. It is measured based on an open question of the type "What international sport organisations do you know?" An individual can reply, for example, the International Olympic Committee, FIBA, UEFA, and so on.

This indicator evaluates memorisation and is expressed as a percentage. Federation X, for example, can have a spontaneous awareness of 40%, which means that of the individuals questioned, 40% cited the name of this federation. The more frequently cited federations would occupy the much-envied position of "top of mind" (figure 1.5).

Unprompted awareness corresponds to the percentage of individuals capable of recognising a sport organisation within a list that includes it. It is necessary to present a list of organisations, including some not connected with sport, and to ask, for example, the following question: "What are the sport organisations you know in this list, knowing that some do not exist?" This indicator makes it possible to appreciate the capacity to recognise the various sport organisations. The number recognised is generally higher than within the framework of spontaneous awareness.

The Interest of Brand Awareness for the Sport Organisation Brand awareness plays a crucial role in determining the consideration set: the small set of brands to which a consumer gives serious attention when making a purchase (Howard and Sheth, 1969; Narayana and Markin, 1975). So, awareness permits someone to consider an organisation when making a decision to become a member. It is, in fact, difficult to participate in Marcialonga for someone unaware of its existence.

Awareness expresses presence in mind. The more a sport organisation's awareness increases, the more it becomes familiar to an individual. This familiarity can be an asset or a handicap depending on the connotations that the individual associates with the organisation. In memory theory, brand awareness is positioned as a vital first step in building the "bundle" of associations that are attached to the brand in memory (Stokes, 1985). The brand is conceptualised as a node in memory, which allows other information about the brand to be "anchored" to it (Aaker, 1991). The conceptualisation of a network of brand associations in memory with the brand as a central core has been put forward by many others (Keller, 1993; Holden, 1993; Holden and Lutz, 1992). Awareness constitutes an anchor for the image. In the Marcialonga case, having international television coverage permits the association of image traits such as important, a reference, and international, which are positive. The effect can also be negative if, for example, violence in a stadium is reported in the media. In this case, the club's awareness grows, but in association with violence.

When awareness of an organisation is associated with positive connotations, it develops into preference. This is above all the case

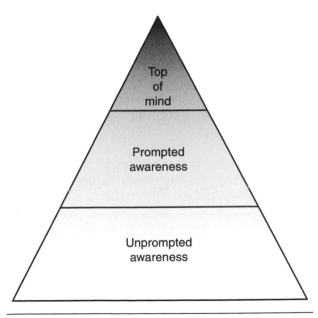

Figure 1.5 From unprompted awareness to top of mind.

when an individual does not perceive major differences between the organisations present. Football, for example, is largely ahead in terms of the sports preferred by children and adolescents. Similarly, judo is often preferred to other combat sports.

The awareness of a sport organisation creates opportunities for sponsoring. We shall develop this aspect in detail in chapter 4.

Brand Image

Referring to Kapferer (1988), image is often assimilated with the cognitive component of attitude. Aaker (1991) uses the term "associations linked to the brand". These are connotations or manifestations referring to the way in which the brand is perceived. When Europeans are asked what the NBA means to them, for example, replies such as "American", "best basketball in the world", "show", "business", and "I love it" are received. If the content of the responses is analysed, we obtain rational factors (high-level basketball, North American professional league, quarter-time, Lakers, Jordan, etc.) and emotional ones (pleasure, I like it, etc.). Image is a very broad concept, and according to Brochand and Lendrevie (2000) it corresponds to "all manifestations, associated by an individual to a brand, an enterprise or an idea".

The structure of the Marcialonga image is presented in table 1.5. The structure and the relationship between variables are determined using a principal factor analysis. The main dimension (factor 1) gathers the following items: "the volunteers", "joyful atmosphere", "warmth of people", "the refreshment points", "efficient organisation", "hospitality", "tradition", "track passing through the villages", and "international focus". The items correlated with the second dimension (factor 2) suggest a challenge with a noncompetitive spirit. The third dimension (factor 3) is related to the winter landscape and the cross-country skiing.

The image of the sport organisation creates value. Aaker (1991) suggests the following:

- Knowledge of the brand image provides useful and even necessary background information when developing a brand identity.
- It helps to summarise a set of facts and specifications providing an important

basis for differentiation. Marcialonga is the Worldloppet race that welcomes everyone.

- It is likely to influence the decision to purchase or make repeat purchases.
- It can create the basis for a sponsorship agreement.
- It can provide the basis for an extension by creating a fit between the brand name and a new product.

It is thus a question of determining the traits of the image that have an impact on the communication target. From a strategic point of view, it is necessary to reinforce the fact that Marcialonga is perceived as friendly, warm, international, challenging to everyone, and well organised. These traits correspond to the core of this brand identity. They must be actively communicated, particularly since they constitute a competitive advantage over other events in Italy and in Europe. In order to select the relevant image dimensions to communicate we suggest the following steps:

1. Diagnostics relating to the image—how is the sport organisation perceived at present?
2. Definition of identity—how does the sport organisation wish to be perceived?
3. Choice of positioning—part of the identity of the sport organisation that must be communicated actively to the various targets, and that reveals a competitive advantage compared with its rivals

Experience

An experience is the sum total of the interactions that a person has with a sport organisation's services, product, people, and processes. It begins from the moment the person gets in touch with the brand and continues through the moment when the person is using the service and beyond. Olympic sport organisation stakeholders have expectations and are looking for satisfaction. This is the first experience outcome. The second refers to service expectations leading to perceived quality.

Satisfaction

Oliver (1997), a respected expert on the topic of satisfaction, expresses the chal-

Table 1.5 **Analysis Into Main Components of Items Relating to the Marcialonga Image**

Items	Means	Factor 1	Factor 2	Factor 3
The volunteers	4.17	0.818*		
Joyful atmosphere	4.24	0.813*		
Warmth of people	4.17	0.783*		
Refreshment points	3.97	0.782*		
Efficient organisation	3.89	0.765*		
Hospitality	4.05	0.702*		
Tradition	4.15	0.689*		
Track passing through the villages	4.21	0.621*		
International focus	3.95	0.559*		
Noncompetitive spirit prevailing over the competitive spirit	3.51		0.783*	
Individual race that makes you feel part of a group	3.69		0.782*	
The "bisons" (the crowd of amateur skiers)	3.91		0.676*	
Same attention given to the winner and to the last classified competitor	3.85		0.66*	
Length of the effort (more time to actually "live" the race)	3.91		0.519*	
Close contact with mountains and nature	3.77			0.876*
Winter landscape	3.58			0.858*
Cross-country skiing	4.13			0.542*
Variance %		40.84	10.41	6.26
Eigenvalue		6.94	1.77	1.07
Factor interpretation		Warmth of people and volunteers mixed with tradition under a good organising umbrella	Challenge with a noncompetitive spirit	Winter landscape and cross-country skiing

*These are correlation coefficients between expectations and dimensions (maximum value = 1).

Reprinted, by permission, from Bazzanella, P, 2003, Developing sport event brand equity: The Marcialonga case. MEMOS dissertation. Université Claude Bernard, Lyon.

lenge of defining this concept: "Satisfaction is the consumer's fulfilment response. It is a judgement that a product or service feature, or the product or service itself, provided (or is providing) a pleasurable level of consumption-related fulfilment, including levels of under or overfulfillment". Nevertheless, the literature reveals significant differences in the definition of satisfaction, although all the definitions share some common elements. Three general components can be identified:

- Consumer satisfaction is a response (emotional or cognitive).
- The response pertains to a particular focus (expectations, product, consumption experience, etc.).
- The response occurs at a particular time (after consumption, after choice, based on accumulated experience, etc.).

Consumer responses follow a general pattern similar to that in the literature. Satisfaction is composed of three basic components—it is a response pertaining to a particular focus determined at a particular time (Giese and Cote, 2000). The complete expectancy disconfirmation with performance model (Oliver, 1997) is consistent with these three characteristics. This model presents a four-step process.

1. A consumer buys a product or a service referring to certain expectations.
2. Experiencing the product or the service, the consumer assesses the performance in relation to each expectation.
3. This process generates a "calculated disconfirmation", based on a rational assessment, and to a "subjective disconfirmation", more emotional and global.
4. This process drives the mental state of satisfaction or dissatisfaction.

It is important to recognise that satisfaction corresponds to the positive psychological state of an individual or entity that expresses, in an explicit or implicit manner, his or her contentment or discontentment following a consumer experience. This consumer experience can be a single one (e.g., participating in a cross-country ski race) or accumulated (belonging to a ski club for a year). This aspect is extremely important when the question is one of evaluating satisfaction. Satisfaction is a dynamic, moving target that may evolve over time, influenced by a variety of factors (Fournier and Mick, 1999). The most important are the following:

- Product and service features
- Consumer emotions

- Attribution for service success or failure
- Perception of equity and fairness
- Other consumers, family members, and coworkers

Moreover, satisfaction has an affective dimension, as the definition expresses, plus a more rational, cognitive dimension linked to the performance of the service compared to expectations.

If it is possible to evaluate only a single parameter, this must be satisfaction. Studies regarding satisfaction are fairly simple to carry out. They make it possible to

- produce an annual satisfaction index,
- measure consumers' expectations,
- measure the perceived performance of products and services compared to expectations,
- understand the motives behind satisfaction and dissatisfaction,
- understand the needs for evolving, and
- define the objectives related to improving quality.

Sport consumers have service expectations. In the Marcialonga case, skiers expect a track in good condition, an organisation ready to immediately meet their requirements and able to provide the services as scheduled, and so on. When and after experiencing the service, skiers are able to assess service performance on each element they expect. This process drives to a calculated disconfirmation because it is based on a rational mode. Participants also use a subjective disconfirmation in order to assess their global experience. This is based on an affective mode. The combination of these two modes creates a state of satisfaction or dissatisfaction.

According to Oliver (1997), satisfaction, in the context of consumption, depends both on the rational assessment results of the consumption and on the emotions accompanying these results and the related events. Oliver points out that the cognitive and emotional aspects of satisfaction may also be in conflict. Thus there may be cognitive satisfaction together with a negative emotional feeling (e.g., my team has won the game and gained points in the championship, but the show was depressing!) or vice versa (my team lost, but played a great game!). Furthermore, the two aspects are not completely separate, and there is always a certain mutual influence. In some cases, there is a complete synergy. Nevertheless, according to Oliver (1997), since satisfaction is a psychological state deriving from a process of emotional and cognitive assessment, a distinction between these two aspects seems necessary in order to explain satisfaction and intentions of behaviour.

The global satisfaction level for the sport service could easily be assessed with the following question:

Globally, what is your opinion about your Marcialonga experience?

- ❑ 6. I am very satisfied.
- ❑ 5. I am satisfied.
- ❑ 4. I am rather satisfied.
- ❑ 3. I am rather unsatisfied.
- ❑ 2. I am unsatisfied.
- ❑ 1. I am very unsatisfied.

Marcialonga Satisfaction Monitoring

The simplest method consists of analysing global satisfaction by producing a satisfaction index on an annual basis (figure 1.6).

Satisfaction indexes must be analysed regularly depending on the segments. The data in figure 1.7 concern two segments based on motives. The main goal of those who are competing is to get the best result (to compete). Those who aim at participating want to complete the race, to be part of the event (to participate). Calculating indexes for these two segments reveals that satisfaction is improving for the competition segment. The participating segment satisfaction rate looks like a V (decreasing and increasing). It is thus worthwhile analysing the causes for this dissatisfaction from a detailed point of view in order to react.

Experiences involve the entire being, provoking emotions. Satisfaction can be considered one of these. An emotion is a subjective, internal experience correlated with a group of physiological reactions arising in response to some situation. In an experience of emotion there is a feeling, or an affective response (e.g., sadness, anger, joy); a physiological response (changes in internal bodily functioning); a cognitive response (an interpretation of the situation); and possibly also a behavioural response (an outward expression).

Sport generates emotions; and participants, spectators, volunteers, and so on are looking for an affective experience. In this context, feeling varies in intensity, ranging from positive to

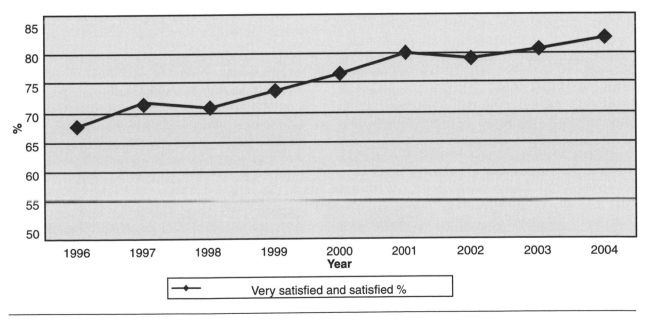

Figure 1.6 Yearly satisfaction index.

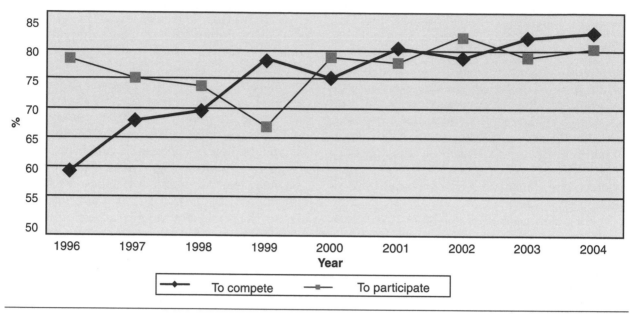

Figure 1.7 Index of global satisfaction based on the motives of the two Marcialonga participant segments.

negative mood states to intense experience. As a marketer you need to provide the right environment and setting for the desired customer experiences to emerge.

Perceived Quality

As suggested by Oliver's (1997) complete expectancy disconfirmation with performance model, satisfaction is the product of an evaluation of the performance of the service supplied as compared with each expectation.

An effective method to assess perceived quality, for example satisfaction cognitive process (calculated disconfirmation), is importance–performance analysis (IPA). This method analyses quality attributes on these two dimensions, which then are combined into a matrix that allows an OSO to identify negative gaps in order to formulate improvement priorities, and to find areas of possible overskill and areas of "acceptable" disadvantages. Through use of the IPA method introduced by Martilla and James (1977), stakeholders are asked to rate each attribute on its performance (five-step scale from very important to not at all important) and on their satisfaction (five-step scale from not at all satisfied to very satisfied). Table 1.6 presents the questionnaire used for Marcialonga participants.

The means of performance and importance divide the matrix (figure 1.8) into four quadrants:

- The area of key success factors corresponds to important expectations for which the service supplied was judged effective (or satisfactory). From a strategic point of view, it is worthwhile reinforcing these aspects.

- The area of conflict consists of important expectations for which the service supplied was judged weak (or unsatisfactory). Priority should be given to intervention regarding these factors, provided that the human, technical, and financial resources are available to do so. This situation can be worrying if competitors offer a more effective service than yours regarding these factors.

- The area relating to the differentiating factors corresponds to expectations of low importance for which the service is judged effective. This is incontestably a positive point, but only moderately favoured by consumers.

- The area corresponding to factors of secondary importance consists of expectations of little importance for which the service has been judged not effective. This information is useful, but it is not worthwhile investing greatly in these points.

As presented earlier, the IPA Marcialonga questionnaire for participants includes 14 items. The structure of Marcialonga participants' expectations is presented in table 1.7. The principal factor analysis determined four factors. Four

Table 1.6 Measuring Marcialonga Participants' Perceived Quality

	IMPORTANT for a cross-country skiing race						SATISFACTION level concerning Marcialonga					
	Absolutely not important 1	Not important 2	Rather important 3	Important 4	Very important 5		Absolutely not satisfied 1	Not very satisfied 2	Rather satisfied 3	Satisfied 4	Extremely satisfied 5	
Ip1	1	2	3	4	5	F1 Modern facilities	1	2	3	4	5	St1
Ip2	1	2	3	4	5	F2 Organisation	1	2	3	4	5	St2
Ip3	1	2	3	4	5	F3 Method of payment	1	2	3	4	5	St3
Ip4	1	2	3	4	5	F4 Quality of the track	1	2	3	4	5	St4
Ip5	1	2	3	4	5	F5 The start	1	2	3	4	5	St5
Ip6	1	2	3	4	5	F6 The friendliness of people	1	2	3	4	5	St6
Ip7	1	2	3	4	5	F7 The course	1	2	3	4	5	St7
Ip8	1	2	3	4	5	F8 The environment	1	2	3	4	5	St8
Ip9	1	2	3	4	5	F9 The snow conditions	1	2	3	4	5	St9
Ip10	1	2	3	4	5	F10 The advertising material for the Marcialonga (magazines and brochures) is pleasant	1	2	3	4	5	St10
Ip11	1	2	3	4	5	F11 Helpfulness of service personnel	1	2	3	4	5	St11

(continued)

Table 1.6 *(continued)*

	IMPORTANT for a cross-country skiing race						F			SATISFACTION level concerning Marcialonga					
	Absolutely not important 1	Not important 2	Rather important 3	Important 4	Very important 5				Absolutely not satisfied 1	Not very satisfied 2	Rather satisfied 3	Satisfied 4	Extremely satisfied 5	
Ip12	1	2	3	4	5	F12 The organisation is ready to immediately meet the requirements of competitors			1	2	3	4	5	St12
Ip13	1	2	3	4	5	F13 The organisation provides services as scheduled			1	2	3	4	5	St13
Ip14	1	2	3	4	5	F14 The main goal of the organising staff is meeting the competitors' requirements at best			1	2	3	4	5	St14

Reprinted, by permission, from Bazzanella, P. 2003. Developing sport event brand equity: The Marcialonga case. MEMOS dissertation. Université Claude Bernard, Lyon.

expectations are strongly correlated with the first factor, which expresses empathy, the capability to reassure, the capability to meet the requirements, and reliability. The second factor refers to concrete elements concerning environmental aspects. The third factor is related to concrete elements having to do with the organisational

aspects. The last concerns another concrete element, that is, the method of payment.

The calculation of the means relative to the importance and the satisfaction for each attribute allows disparity. It is much easier to show the results in the form of a graph. The results for the participants are presented in figure 1.9.

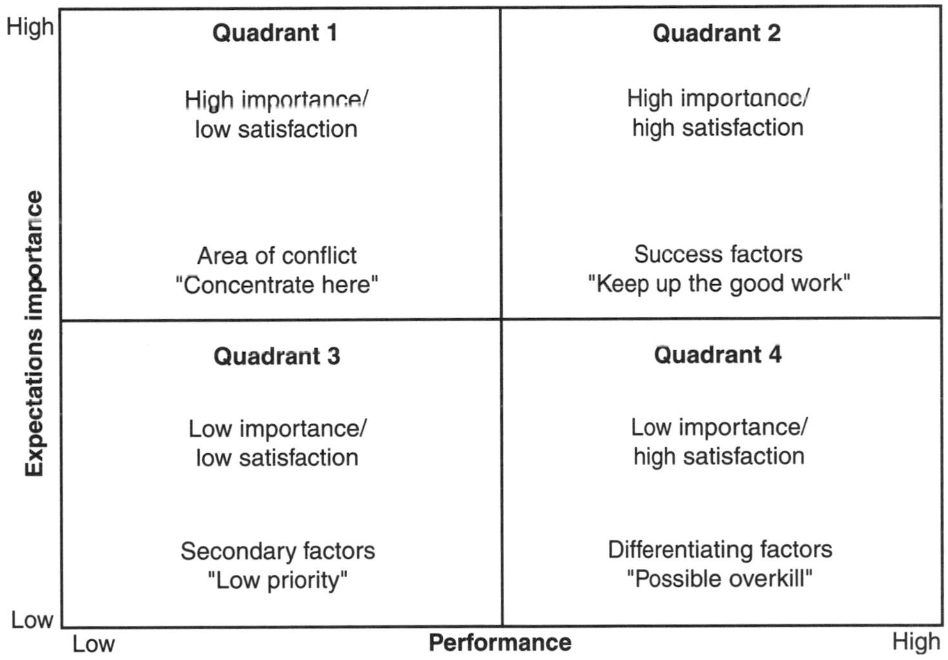

Figure 1.8 Matrix of the relative extent of expectations versus perceived performance.

Table 1.7 **Marcialonga Service Expectations (Principal Factor Analysis)**

Expectations (attributes)	Means	Factor 1	Factor 2	Factor 3	Factor 4
12 The organisation is ready to immediately meet the requirements of competitors	4,06	0.838*			
11 Helpfulness of service personnel	4,17	0.810*			
13 The organisation provides the services as scheduled	4,19	0.788*			
14 The main goal of the organising staff is meeting the competitors' requirements at best	4,21	0.761*			
7 The course	4,28		0.798*		
8 The environment	4,17		0.751*		
9 The snow conditions	4,32		0.591*		

(continued)

Table 1.7 *(continued)*

Expectations (attributes)	Means	Factor 1	Factor 2	Factor 3	Factor 4
10 The ML advertising material is pleasant	3,48		0.590*		
4. Quality of the track	4,64			0.780*	
2. Organisation	4,50			0.705*	
5. The start	4,39			0.603*	
1. Modern equipment	3,96			0.568*	
3. Method of payment	3,64				0.859*
Variance %		34.571	9.593	8.824	7.686
Eigenvalue		4.840	1.343	1.235	1.076
Factor interpretation		Empathy, capability to reassure, capability to meet the requirements, and reliability	Concrete elements related to the environment	Concrete elements related to the organisation	Method of payment

*These are correlation coefficients between expectations and dimensions (maximum value = 1).

Reprinted, by permission, from Bazzanella, P. 2003. Developing sport event brand equity: The Marcialonga case. MEMOS dissertation. Université Claude Bernard, Lyon.

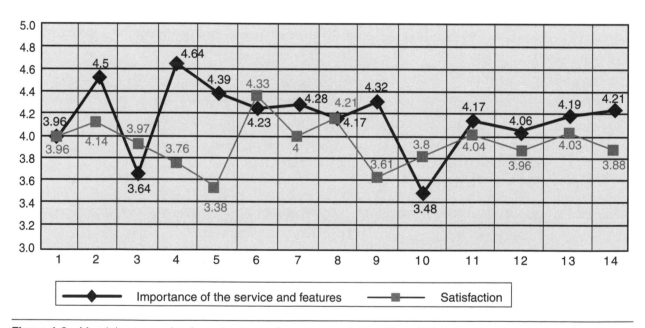

Figure 1.9 Marcialonga service importance–performance analysis with participants.

Reprinted, by permission, from Bazzanella, P. 2003. Developing sport event brand equity: The Marcialonga case. MEMOS dissertation. Université Claude Bernard, Lyon.

The upper line refers to the importance attached by the participant to specific services offered by the event. The lower line refers to the grey scale to the left and indicates the satisfaction level for each service attribute. This comparison helps one to visualise the gaps.

N.2. The organisation: Compared to the great importance attached to this aspect, there are reasons for disappointment, even though the gap is slight.

N.4. Quality of the track: This is the most important concrete aspect according to interviewees. In this sense, there is a deficiency in the customers' satisfaction.

N.5. The start: The same applies to this aspect; in comparison with the great importance attached to this element, there is a rather marked dissatisfaction among the interviewees.

N.9. The snow conditions: For this concrete element, too, there is a gap between the importance given and the satisfaction level.

It is possible to use a qualitative method based on interviews. Each person is invited to indicate both unsatisfactory and satisfactory service elements. It is then a question of classifying the responses per topic in order to calculate the frequency. This leads to the results in table 1.8.

Table 1.8 **Reasons for Dissatisfaction on the Part of Members of a Tennis Club**

Number of times quoted	
225	More commitment to members
80	The staff should be more accessible
71	Suggestions should be borne in mind
52	The staff should be more present
24	The staff should be more motivated
120	Improving the quality of the sport service
92	Improving the quality of the courts
28	Increasing the number of training sessions
92	**Reduction in prices**

These results can be presented in the form of a Paretto graph in order to visualise the progression curve (see figure 1.10). In the example shown, the first three reasons, which represent 78% of the total, should be borne in mind.

The analysis must be followed by proposals for evolution and the reasons for satisfaction. Figure 1.11 (fictitious example) shows six motives that should be considered.

Studies on satisfaction make it possible to carry out regular diagnostics. These are fairly easy to do, and correspond to the pretest phase described for the process relating to the conception of a new service.

From an operational point of view, the following must be evaluated:

1. Whether what is offered corresponds to demand. For this, you can use the matrix for expectations versus perceived performance, or ask for motives for dissatisfaction, needs for evolution, and motives for satisfaction. It is, however, absolutely essential to intervene on the factors located in the area of conflict (provided that the capacity and the means are available).

2. The performance by your competition compared with your offer. Analysing the performance of offers by competitors, if these exist, is an essential strategic factor. It is fairly difficult to obtain information on this, for you must ask questions of competitors' members or of consumers who know or have used their services. According to Aaker (1991), "Perceived quality is the idea that a consumer develops of the quality of a product or a service depending

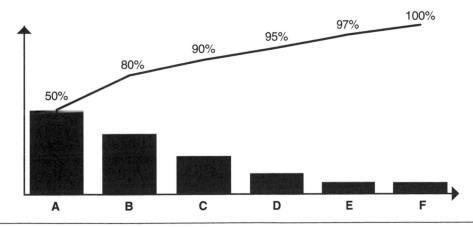

Figure 1.10 Paretto graph relating to reasons for dissatisfaction.

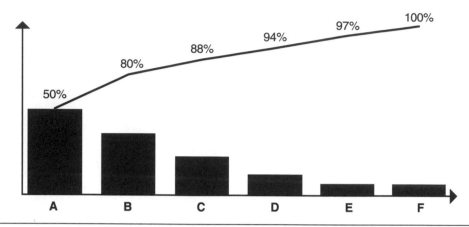

Figure 1.11 Paretto graph relating to reasons for satisfaction.

on his expectations and the comparisons that he can make with competing brands".

Assessing and Managing Stakeholder Quality

The IPA method aims at managing quality based on the perceived gaps. We go into this in more detail in connection with the analysis and management of the quality of services for a sport organisation. Between 1985 and 1988, Parasuraman, Zeithaml, and Berry developed a model that made it possible to analyse the gaps that the organisation must bridge in order to improve the quality of its service. This famous model considers five gaps.

FIVE GAPS ORGANISATIONS MUST OVERCOME

1. Gap Between the Perceived Service and Expected Service

This gap is related to the two stakeholder questions. Stakeholders are evaluating OSO service performance in relation to their expectations. If the stakeholders are rational, this assessment determines their satisfaction. It is named the *consumer gap.* Two questions are relevant to assess this gap:

1. What is the service our stakeholders expect from us?
2. How do they assess the quality of our service?

2. Gap Between Stakeholders' Expectations and the Perception of These Expectations by OSO

Managers often have the wrong idea of the expectations of those for whom the service is intended. At times, they do not even ask themselves what these expectations are. In this context, only a specific study makes it possible to determine the expectations. OSOs must reduce this gap in order to construct a long-term relationship with their members and partners. Two questions are relevant to assess this gap:

1. What is the service our stakeholders expect from us?
2. How are we perceiving our stakeholders' expectations?

3. Gap Between the Perception of Expectations by OSO and Expressing These As Quality Standards

Whatever the expected perception of OSO staff stakeholders is, it is necessary to express these as quality standards. Here, it is a question of formalising these standards by drawing up procedures and performance criteria (e.g., deciding to handle any request for information within 24 hours). It should be noted that these standards should be within the capacity of the organisation. Two questions are relevant to assess this gap:

1. How are we perceiving our stakeholders' expectations?
2. How are we translating our perceptions into service specifications?

4. Gap Between the Quality Standards and the Service Supplied

Stakeholders wish to obtain a service that is in line with their expectations. The sport organisation must certainly develop plans for this service, but they must also be capable of supplying it. There are many obstacles: training the staff, equipment, availability, and so on. Two questions are relevant to assess this gap:

1. How are we translating our perceptions into service specifications?
2. What is our service perceived performance?

5. Gap Between the Service Provided and the External Communications

External communication (e.g., publicity, flyers) involves promises relating to the capacity of the service to satisfy a certain number of expectations. This influences the expectations of clients, who are all the more frustrated if the service supplied does not correspond to what has been promised. Two questions are relevant to assess this gap:

1. What is our service perceived performance?
2. Which promise are we communicating to our stakeholders?

The gap relating to the consumer constitutes the essential point of this model. It concerns the difference between the expected service and the perceived service that determines the satisfaction from a rational point of view. The organisation must reduce this gap in order to construct a long-term relationship with its members and partners. In this perspective, the model suggests that it is necessary to also reduce the other four gaps related to the supplier (provider gaps). These stress the causes behind the gap linked to the consumer.

Gap 2: Not knowing what consumers expect

Gap 3: Not offering the right kind of service

Gap 4: Not delivering a service

Gap 5: Not matching performance to promises

This tool has been criticised and improved. Cronin and Taylor (1992) contest the notion of quality and prefer that of satisfaction. They have developed the SERVPERF model, which proposes a measurement scale that can differ according to sectors of activity and is based on performance. We, however, consider that its main contribution is to relate the importance of expectations to performance. In our opinion, its main limitation is linked to the fact that it is not specific to a sport organisation. It is, nevertheless, important for a sport organisation to understand what actually drives its stakeholders' satisfaction in order to enhance the quality of service supplied. We generally use the term "total quality management" to stress this process that is both precise and systematic.

The quality cycle (figure 1.12) is intended to reduce possible gaps. The first is the gap between expected and perceived quality. A Marcialonga participant wishes to have a warm welcome, some relevant information, a good track, and so forth. The participant is looking for quality, for example to receive a service that fulfils his

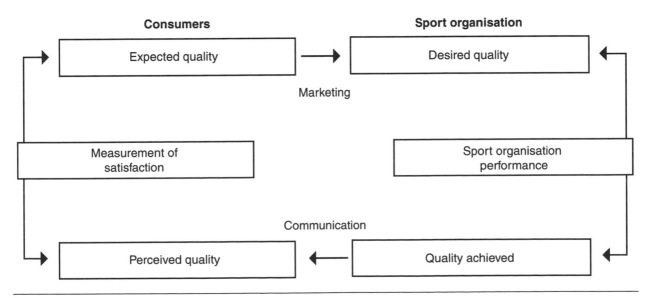

Figure 1.12 The quality cycle.

or her expectations. The person's event experience will allow him or her to assess the service quality, for example perceived quality. This is a key factor: It is the consumer who appreciates the perceived quality in comparison with the quality that individual expects. Satisfaction results from this evaluation.

Total quality management constitutes an essential competitive strategy for sport organisations. A marketing approach makes it possible to analyse the consumers' current and future expectations. Answers should be supplied to the following questions: Why do people practise sport? What do they want? When? Where? In what form?

Service that satisfies all expectations rarely exists because it must be profitable from an economic point of view and must be feasible. It is therefore necessary to make choices by concentrating on satisfying the most important expectations. It is not possible to invest lots of money in a snow-making system in order to guarantee an optimum track.

The perceived quality influences satisfaction, which in turn influences loyalty. This chain of dependency is presented in figure 1.13.

This is particularly true when the sport organisation is seeking to develop within a competitive context. The importance of client satisfaction in a competitive context has been demonstrated by numerous studies. Nevertheless, the relation between satisfaction and loyalty depends on the extent of competition in the sector. Thus, when the sport organisation has a monopoly or is situated in a sector with little competition, the members can be completely dissatisfied yet remain loyal. This is the case of persons wishing to practise competitively, or professional clubs with their governing federa-

tion. Other factors also come into play such as the high value of the brand and the relative cost of changing it. When the sector becomes more competitive, those who are dissatisfied have other alternatives. When the market becomes highly competitive, as is the case for fitness, it becomes difficult to conserve satisfied individuals. This is reinforced by low differentiation of the offer, low commitment on the part of the consumer, and a low cost of changing.

Relationship

Stakeholders have a relationship with the OSO brand. Indeed, the brand is often at the crux of transactions and exchanges between organisations and people. A relationship characterises some sort of connection between two or more people or organisations. A relationship has three dimensions: content, duration, and intensity.

- Content refers to the nature of the expectations fulfilled (functional, emotional, social, etc.) in the exchange.
- Duration refers to the length.
- Intensity refers to frequency and involvement.

From a marketing perspective it is crucial to act with the conscious aim of developing and managing relationships with OSO stakeholders that are long term or trusting, or both. This relationship could be based on personal involvement (volunteers, participants, spectators, etc.) or could be a business relationship based on a contract. In this context, loyalty is an important indicator of marketing performance. From a business perspective it can be reinforced through developing a relationship marketing strategy.

Loyalty

We begin with loyalty, since this is the veritable key to marketing action. We have stressed that offensive marketing is aimed at motivating new consumers or at taking them from the competition, and that defensive marketing seeks to make them loyal. Loyalty makes it possible to develop a feeling of commitment to the brand among its "clients". For example, certain football clubs have neglected their supporters in order to invest in programmes aimed

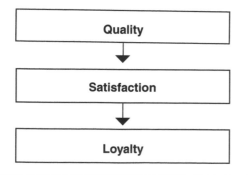

Figure 1.13 Relations between perceived quality, satisfaction, and loyalty.

at attracting new clients.[7] However, it is often very difficult to win over new clients who have few reasons to change brands (supporters above all). It is also costly to create awareness among this type of client, who makes little effort to come to you. Conserving existing clients, on the other hand, is highly profitable. First, it costs less because a reduction, even a slight one, in the loss rate of clients is rapidly expressed by an increase in sales. Even without major effort, new clients will arrive, and current clients will have influenced some.

To illustrate the importance of loyalty for a sport organisation, we can take the example of two national federations that each have 10% new members each year. The first loses 5% of its members per year, while the second loses 10%. After 14 years, the first federation will have doubled the number of its licensed members while the second will have the same number. A client base is like a leaking bucket: It is better to repair the hole than to wear oneself out trying to fill it.

The Marcialonga case is specific due to the limitation of participant numbers. Indeed, the organisation cannot manage safety and quality for more than 5,000 people. Most of the "participation" marathons limit participant numbers. Data presented table 1.9 demonstrate a high level of loyalty from 1996 to 2002. During the last two years the organisation decided to give the priority to foreign participants.

Aaker (1991) distinguishes five levels of loyalty to a brand. Each level raises a different marketing problem.

- The committed buyer is frequent in sport organisations. This is a militant who promotes the organisation by word of mouth.
- The second level corresponds to a person who likes the brand and has an emotional link to it corresponding to the affective dimension of attitude.
- The third level corresponds to a person with a rational approach. This person is satisfied given that the brand satisfies his or her expectations.
- The fourth level corresponds to a person who is a regular buyer, more or less satisfied, and who has no major reasons for changing.
- The last level corresponds to individuals who are little or not at all sensitive to the brand. Here, the price is the essential criterion, and these buyers will change if they find something similar less expensive elsewhere.

This classification takes into account the three dimensions of measurement of loyalty.

Table 1.9 **Marcialonga Participant Loyalty Rate**

Years	Participants	New participants	Loyalty %
1996	4,398	1,268	71.17%
1997	4,246	1,204	71.64%
1998	4,800	1,350	71.87%
1999	4,293	1,140	73.45%
2000	4,722	1,377	70.84%
2001	4,205	999	76.24%
2002	4,198	955	77.25%
2003	5,048	2,268	55.07%
2004	4,296	1,453	66.18%

[7] Associations of supporters who are long-standing subscribers criticise their eviction from the spectator stands in favour of creating VIP and business seats. Nantes Football Club, for example, tripled its subscription to the presidential stand for the 2001-2002 season after winning the French championship.

We presented tools that make it possible to measure these dimensions in the section on consumer behaviour.

Among the advantages cited by Aaker (1991), we retain three that directly concern a sport organisation.

1. Loyalty reduces marketing expenditure because it is much less costly to conserve members than to win new ones.

2. Loyalty makes it possible to win new members because the presence of loyal consumers is perceived as a guarantee of quality. Moreover, these members promote the brand by word of mouth.

3. Loyalty makes it easier to defend oneself against attacks by competitors. Satisfied members do not necessarily seek another service. Moreover, change implies a cost and a risk.

Stakeholders

Stakeholder number and characteristics are one aspect of brand equity. Indeed, Marcialonga S.c.a.r.l. and Ski Club Marcialonga gather 5,000 participants, volunteers, local authorities (Trentino region, etc.), and sponsors. This constitutes a large network source with a strong social impact in this area. The second aspect, which is the most important, refers to the structure and the nature of these relationships.

According to Parvatiyar and Sheth (2000), relationship marketing is "the ongoing process of engaging in cooperative and collaborative activities and programmes with immediate and end-user customers to create or enhance mutual economic value at reduced cost". Three underlying dimensions of relationship formation are suggested by this definition: parties, purpose, and programmes (figure 1.14).

- Parties (stakeholders). Parties refers to the stakeholders involved in the relationship programme. As a sport event, Marcialonga is the main programme. There are subprogrammes such as the Trentino Open Village involving the organising committee, sponsors, media, and local authorities.

- Purpose. The overall purpose of relationship marketing is to improve marketing effectiveness and enhance values for the parties by seeking and achieving strategic marketing goals and their mission.

- Programmes. These are the visible and operational dimensions. All parties share their resources and competencies in order to create a competitive advantage.

The Trentino Open Village is a village built around the finish line and visited in the days before the race and on the day of Marcialonga 2005 (table 1.10). Some 30,000 visitors a day will get this unique "experience".

The organising committee was in search of new creative ideas in order to build a closer and mutually beneficial relationship with its stakeholders. The Trentino Open Village will

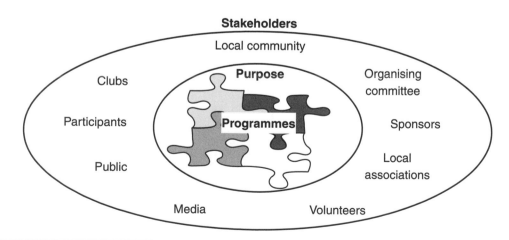

Figure 1.14 The three dimensions of relationship formation.

Table 1.10 **Parties Involved in the Trentino Open Village**

Parties involved (stakeholders)	Goals and benefits (purpose)	Service delivered (contribution)
Tourist council (Trentino S.p.A.)	To promote local facilities	Promotion Information point Inflatable structure
Province of Trentino and municipalities	To promote local facilities	Promotion Information point
Ca'Vit	To promote their products	Self-testing and games
Trentingrana	To promote their products	Self-testing and games
Casse Rurali Trentine	To promote their services (bank and insurance)	Information point and games
Melinda	To promote their products	Self-testing and games
Media, radio and TV	To involve audience with regard to authentic products	Programmes (radio and TV live)
Visitors	To taste and have fun	None

be the first relationship marketing programme associated with Marcialonga. The committee will reach the first stage in 2005 and intends to develop this initiative in order to create a competitive advantage and to create a network. In the following we can see the stages relating to the evolution of a relational marketing strategy. In an OSO, relationship marketing can be developed in three stages. Each one corresponds to a new step. In this process, commitment and trust develop and lead to cooperation.

- Stage 1: Building relationships. Recognising the value that can be delivered from the economic and resource content of relationships, managers seek out relationship partners who are socially compatible. Those relationships that are important for OSO success and characterised by social compatibility are especially nurtured. Olympic sport organisations should take the initiative of building cooperation programmes involving existing stakeholders and of recruiting new ones.
- Stage 2: Creating a competitive advantage based on these relationships. Each party involved has resources and competencies.

These are combined with the OSO's own resources. A competitive advantage is created based on superior resources and competencies.

- Stage 3: Network development. Ultimately, relationship marketing strategy leads to cooperative value networks. These should be perpetuated.

Relationship marketing is an important asset for OSOs. It attempts to involve and integrate the stakeholders. It assumes overlap in the plans and process of the interacting parties and suggests close economic, emotional, and structural bonds among them.

1.3 Conclusion

Despite its business connotation, managing the brand is a crucial issue for a non-profit-making organisation. It brings value to the OSO and to its stakeholders. In this particular context, we stress two important issues linked to brand management. The first concerns brand management itself, and the second refers to brand extensions.

Brand Strategy

We developed a method based on six dimensions: foundation, legal protection, knowledge, experience, relationship, and stakeholders (FLKERS). The method consists of managing the brand from a firm base. For certain OSOs it is about the building of foundations for their brand and associating their brand with a certain number of events and programmes. A brand takes the form of a symbol constructed in order to represent a collection of information about events, programmes, and initiatives. This symbolic construct must be associated into the target's mind. Numerous OSOs are not associated with the events that they organise. They have bonded their corporate brand with the event brand, such as UCI Mountain Bike World Cup, FIVB World League, UEFA EURO 2004™, and so on. From a strategic point of view they took advantage of the existing relationship between the event and the audience, and they reinforce the relationship and trigger recognition with consistent brand name and visual symbols.

A relevant brand name should be legally protectable, be easy to pronounce, be easy to remember, be easy to recognise, attract attention, suggest product benefits (functional, emotional, social, etc.), and position the OSO and the event relative to the competition. Some situations are complex. Two countries hosted the FIFA 2002 World Cup. FIFA was looking for an emblem to represent the host countries of Korea and Japan with the following specifications: one that would be accepted by international culture, be creative and appropriate for merchandising and media, maintain FIFA's unique brand identity, and communicate the spirit of unity embodied by the world's most popular sport. They asked for the support of Interbrand[8] to create this emblem.

This proliferation of brands in a single organisation raises some strategic questions. Is a specific brand accurate? How can overlapping brands avoid undermining each other? How can the confusion factor be reduced? Which role does each brand play is this system?

In such a complex environment, the key management principle is to consider the brands as a system. The overall purpose is to create superior value for each one and for the whole system. A brand system has five objectives (Aaker, 1996):

- To exploit commodities to generate strategy
- To reduce brand identity damage
- To achieve clarity of product on offer
- To facilitate change and adaptation
- To allocate resources

As illustrated with FIFA, brands in this system fall into a natural hierarchy. Each one has a natural role to play. Aaker (1996) provides an overview of the roles that brands can play in a system. Olympic sport organisations are developing different kinds of brands (see table 1.11).

Each type of brand has a role with reference to the OSO's strategy.

1. The corporate brand represents the OSO with people, culture, values, and programmes and has an endorser role. It provides support and credibility to the driver brand's claims. In our example, FIFA is an endorser for 2006 FIFA World Cup Germany. As an endorser brand, FIFA brings a certain guarantee and ethic to the sub-brand (see definition below).

2. A driver brand represents the value proposition, which influences the purchase decision. For example, with the 2006 FIFA World Cup Germany, sponsors are primarily buying the audience and the FIFA values. These are presented in table 1.12. As a result, the World Cup is the driver brand, and its name and symbol need to have a strong and clear identity.

3. A sub-brand is a brand that distinguishes a part of the product line within the brand system. The product or the service is closely related to other brands or the overall corporate brand. For example, FIFA is developing a large sub-brand range: The brands have different roles in FIFA's strategy. For example, FIFA is using the sub-brand World Cup to distinguish a specific event from others. FIFA World Cup reinforces FIFA leadership as a governing body. It is a strategic brand because it is important to the performance of the organisation. As a large and dominant brand, the World Cup is able to

---

[8] www.interbrand.com

Table 1.11 **Main Brand Types Used by OSOs**

Types of brand	Characteristics	Examples in the soccer sector
Corporate brand	• Represents the OSO as the brand; should reflect the organisation culture, values, and practices. • OSOs are using their corporate brand as an umbrella because its appears on a number of products that may each have separate brand images.	FIFA, UEFA, Real Madrid
Driver brand	• Value proposition, which influences the purchase decision.	With the 2006 FIFA World Cup Germany, sponsors are primarily buying the audience and the FIFA values
Sub-brand	• A brand that distinguishes a part of the product line within the brand system • A sub-brand could be employed as a vehicle for changing or supporting the brand image of a parent or corporate brand. In this case it is named silver bullet brand.	• FIFA World Cup • The FIFA sub-brand's ranges reinforce some FIFA values, for example trust, solidarity, democracy, quality, and universality.

Table 1.12 **2002 FIFA World Cup Audience and FIFA Values**

2002 FIFA World Cup Audience	FIFA values
• Television coverage in 213 countries and over 41,100 hours of programming—a 38% increase over 1998. • A cumulative in-home audience of 28.8 billion viewers. • Live audiences were not affected by the time zone differences for viewers in Europe and Central and South America. • Proper, audited research for China introduced for the first time, which accounted for a 14% reduction in the global audience total when compared to 1998. Taking China out of the equation, the global figure is actually up 2%.	"The house of FIFA" represents a shared vision for the future of FIFA and reflects the following values: • Trust • Solidarity • Democracy • Quality • Universality

increase and maintain FIFA's position (driver role). The FIFA Futsal World Championship is consistent with the FIFA mission. It facilitates a horizontal extension strategy by qualifying the FIFA corporate brand, exploiting market opportunities, and prescribing the game.

4. A silver bullet is a sub-brand that is employed as a vehicle for changing or supporting the brand image of a parent or corporate brand. The FIFA sub-brand ranges reinforce some FIFA values, for example trust, solidarity, democracy, quality, and universality.

Branding benefits can help with a problem facing many brands, which is that their identity is difficult to communicate because it lacks distinctiveness, credibility, or memorability. The solution may lie in branding features, components, or service programmes that provide customer benefits. For example, FIFA is running the FIFA Goal Programme aimed at rebuilding football in Afghanistan. Football can unite people. This action reinforces FIFA identity consistency regarding solidarity and universalism. A branded benefit feature, component, or service can also play a silver bullet role by supporting the image of the brand to which it is attached. Thus it can do more than help communicate a functional benefit.

Brand Extension

Brand extension is another challenge for OSOs. Brand extension consists in using an established brand name to launch a different product or service, in a product category that differs from the initial product category (Aaker and Keller, 1990; Farquart, 1990; Kapferer, 1998). These authors make the distinction between brand extension (launching in a different product category) and brand line extension (launching a slightly different item in the same product category). Familiar brand extensions for an OSO are merchandised or licensed products. This seems to be an easy way of capitalising on an OSO brand's equity to sell new products or services.

We suggest that brand extension should be analysed taking into account the end user's perception. This person uses a psychological process referred to as emotional attitude transfer—"I like the FIFA World Cup, I like its licensed products", for example official mascot cuddly, T-shirts, ties, watches, pens, pins, and cups. According to FIFA, these products are an "effective means for fans to indulge their passion for a sporting event. Both enable fans to feel that they are part of the action and to declare their support for the event as a whole. The FIFA World Cup Licensing Programme[9] offers the millions of enthusiastic fans a wide range of high-quality Official Licensed Products to choose from". Aaker and Keller (1990) proposed an attitude-based brand extension model in which several factors influence the success of extension. For an OSO there are obvious benefits of pursuing a brand extension strategy such as business growth, cementing core brand attributes, and promoting the event and OSO brand[10]. There are also significant downsides of a brand extension strategy in that if a brand extension does not fit with the core brand, the core brand may not add any value to the brand extension product or service, resulting in the failure of the brand extension; core brand attributes may well be diluted, and negative attributes may be associated with the core brand. In many organisations today one finds a proliferation of brands and brand extensions and a bewildering set of overlapping and sometimes inconsistent brand roles. It is crucial to develop a brand strategy.

Managing the OSO brand needs to be consistent with some generic principles. Interbrand[11]has developed some of these, and we like to stress those most relevant for an OSO:

- "Branding can be applied to anything from products and services to companies, non-profit-making concerns and even countries".

- "Brands can also have a critical social importance and benefits in both developed and developing countries. This applies as much to commercial brands as not-for-profit organisations".

- "Every brand, if it is to be successful, needs a clear positioning, expressed through name, identity and all the aspects of products, services and behaviour".

- "Increasingly, brands require a distinctive customer experience in the round".

---

[9] www.fifa.com

[10] Market research conducted by FIFA marketing and TV in 13 countries proved that the FIFA World Cup marks are now more valuable than ever. The FIFA World Cup trophy was immediately recognised by 90% of those interviewed and the 2002 World Cup official emblem by 61%.

[11] www.interbrand.com

two

Understanding the Olympic Sport Organisation's Target Audience

Marketing is centred on the consumer. In this context, it is essential to understand and analyse the process that leads the consumer to make or repeat a purchase. Within the framework of the marketing of services, the strategy can be either defensive or offensive. The defensive strategy aims to create loyalty among members, who are its "clients". It is based on the satisfaction of expectations, which is a key point. An offensive strategy aims to recruit new members into the marketplace. Competition has to be considered. It can be direct or indirect. If we refer to "sport as an object", sport organisations find themselves in direct competition in order to recruit new members or to obtain sport sponsoring. If we refer to expectations (self-accomplishment, pleasure, making friends, etc.), sport organisations are in competition with leisure activities in general. In this context it is worthwhile not only to identify the expectations of the various marketing targets (the persons to whom the service is offered), but also to understand and analyse their decision-making processes. In fact, a certain number of such processes exist, and we shall examine these. This will make it possible to orient the marketing activities and its variables (service, price, distribution, communication) in a way that will be more effective than that of the competition.

The various areas of operational marketing that we presented in the introduction permit us to identify the marketing targets for sport organisations. We shall retain the two following target categories:

- Individuals looking for a service that fulfils their expectations
- Organisations aiming to fulfil their business needs (media, sponsor, etc.; making a deal is a job) or a social need (NPO).

There are two marketing outcomes:

- Securing the members' loyalty (defensive marketing)
- Recruiting people or organisations (offensive marketing)

The section that follows is a fairly conceptual one that makes use of illustration. First we analyse the decision-making process on the part of the consumer. Here we present the essential variables with a view to expanding on this model. Secondly we carry out a typology related to these processes. Finally we stress the importance of emotional processes in the case of consuming sport services. This approach gave rise to the development of the experiential marketing concept.

EXHIBIT 2.1 FÉDÉRATION INTERNATIONALE DE VOLLEY BALL

The FIVB is the worldwide leader in innovative "new-generation" sport entertainment:

- One of the top three global international sporting federations
- Provides leadership to 500 million players
- Provides leadership to 33 million licensed athletes
- Has 218 affiliated national federations
- Awards over US$ 25 million in prize money every year
- Partners with up to 100 event organisers and TV broadcasters annually

The Game

The game consists of two major disciplines, volleyball and beach volleyball, and is a dynamic sport played by two teams on a playing court divided by a net. Continuous rally scoring maintains spectator excitement and game drama.

Volleyball is played indoors with six players per side. Beach volleyball is played outdoors on sand with two players per side.

Properties

- Volleyball: World Championship, World League, World Cup, and World Grand Prix
- Beach volleyball: World Tour and World Championship

Source: www.fivb.com

2.1 Understanding the Audience in Order to Provide a Positive Experience

"There will always, one can assume, be a need for some selling. But the aim of marketing is to make selling superfluous. The aim of marketing is to know and understand the customer so well that the product or service fits him and sells itself. Ideally marketing should result in a customer who is ready to buy. All that should be needed then is to make the product or service available". (Peter Drucker, 1990)

The marketing process starts with the consumer in the marketplace and aims to make profits (social, financial, or both) through satisfaction. For OSOs, the problem lies in the gap between this commercial focus and their social mission. They are acting to "contribute to building a peaceful and better world by educating youth through sport practised without discrimination of any kind and in the Olympic spirit" (IOC), "to develop and promote all aspects of cycling without discrimination of any kind" (UCI). . . . They aim at influencing humans' behaviour on a large scale in order to improve their personal welfare and that of their society through sport. In this context, when OSOs are acting in a competitive market, for example, when they have to manage sponsorship, profits made by commercial marketing secure financial issues for social marketing.[1]

The research aiming to analyse consumer behaviour has permitted the establishment of some models explaining the consumer decision-making process. These models situate the variables influencing this process as well as their relationship. There are different stages in the history of consumer behaviour. The first models appeared during the period of 1966 to 1972, with the grand theories by Andreasen (1965), Nicosia (1966), Howard and Sheth (1969), and Engel, Kollat, and Blackwell (1968). The information-processing approach is based on Fishbein and Ajzen's theory of attitude and an information-processing theory. In the 1980s the affective approach stressed the importance of emotion and building the foundation for the experiential approach (1900s) highlighting the symbolic meaning of consumption, hedonism, and expressive value. In this section we stress the main variables to consider in order to understand sport consumer behaviour. From this perspective, Assael's (1998) simple model of consumer behaviour identifies four main areas to consider and their relationship. We

---

[1] The Olympic movement receives most of its funding from the Olympic Games rights bought by broadcast networks. However, it also benefits from the Olympic Partners (TOP) worldwide sponsorship programme comprising multinational companies. The IOC distributes 92% of the revenue generated by the marketing of Olympic properties. www.olympic.org/uk/organisation/facts/revenue/index_uk.asp.

recommend this book for those who want to go through the details.

The central part of this book refers to consumer decision making determining the consumer response. In a marketing perspective we have to consider two kinds of decisions. The first is related to loyalty. The second kind of decision refers to recruiting people in a competitive marketplace. We present a decision-making typology and describe the dynamics of this process.

Consumer decision making is influenced both by individual and by environmental characteristics.

- The individual consumer can be analysed considering demographics, needs, motives, personality, attitudes, and lifestyle. With a focus on sport consumers we consider five variables: motives, involvement, attitude, loyalty, and lifestyle.

- Environmental influences refer to the consumer's purchasing environment represented by culture (norms and values of society), by subcultures, and by face-to-face groups (friends, family members, and reference groups). Marketing organisations are part of the environment and try to influence the decision-making process. We narrow our focus, highlighting the influence of reference groups, opinion leaders, and culture.

Once the consumer has made a decision, he or she gets into a consumption experience. This leads to two forms of feedback. One form is directed to the consumer him- or herself. The consumer learns from this experience, and the process can affect the individual's motives and attitudes. The second form of feedback leads back to the environment. Sport consumers communicate about experience to friends and family. This communication can affect the environment.

Let's get into this "black box" and specify the main variables to be considered.

The Individual Sport Consumer

In order to understand a consumer's behaviour, it is relevant to examine the relationship between a certain number of variables and the consumer. Here, we develop the most important of these variables: motives, attitude, involvement, and loyalty.

Motives

Ascertaining the factors that motivate individuals to consume a sport, or managers to get involved in sponsorship, is a crucial and complex issue. Motivation is the driving force behind all actions of an organism. The AMA defines consumer motivation as "the needs, wants, drives, and desires of an individual that lead him or her towards the purchase of products or ideas. The motivations may be physiologically, psychologically, or environmentally driven". The motivational drive directly affects the specific benefit criteria used to evaluate the OSO brand offer.

Most of the research on motivation for sport consumption, for example that of Sloan (1989) and Wann, Schrader, and Wilson (1999), stresses the fact that motives for sport consumption are varied and multidimensional. The authors group motives into broad classifications. Wann (1995) developed the Sport Motivation Scale, structured according to eight dimensions:

1. Eustress (positive levels of arousal or stress release—"I get pumped when watching my favourite teams")
2. Entertainment (desire to be entertained by sports)
3. Self-esteem (or personal enhancement)
4. Escape (diversion from everyday life)
5. Affiliation needs (to be part of a group)
6. Economic gains (offered via sport, such as wagering)
7. Family motives (to spend time with family members)
8. Aesthetic value of sports ("I consume sport for the artistic value")

Making a decision about a sponsorship operation is a job for a sponsor. The motives match the marketing objectives. We identify commercial and corporate goals.

Commercial objectives aim at selling more products or goods. Companies intend to reach this goal through the following means:

- Increased brand and product awareness
- Demonstrating product or service performance
- Providing credibility to their brand or products

- Building image in the marketplace
- Stimulating their distribution network
- Stimulating their sale force
- Developing goodwill and positive attitude towards the brand
- Increasing sales and market share
- Developing business-to-business relationships

Corporate objectives are aimed at promoting sponsor social values and performance in order to do one or more of the following:

- Reassure stockholders and the financial world
- Demonstrate the company's citizenship and legitimate its social performance
- Promote company culture
- Reinforce internal cohesion and stimulate company staff involvement
- Enhance staff recruitment

Analysing the content of both sport consumers and sponsor motives, we can group them into four main types.

- **Utility and functional motives (cognitive).** These refer to the utility value of the product or service. "I play beach volleyball in order to make technical progress in the sport and to develop my physical capacities". Most of the sponsor commercial motives are rational—for example, to develop brand awareness, to increase sales.

- **Psychological motives.** These correspond to motives of self-expression, evasion, idealisation, and being in control. We are touching on individual motives and the imaginary: "I feel fast, strong, and free playing beach volleyball". Sponsors' psychological motives are related to their staff—for example, to stimulate the sales force, reinforce staff involvement.

- **Social and cultural motives.** Here, the associated benefits bring with them added value of a social and cultural nature. Table tennis is, in this case, the sign of an active, enterprising lifestyle. It is convivial and popular in the correct sense of the term; that is, it is open to all and makes it easy to form real friendships. A sponsor can aim at promoting specific values and company culture.

- **Affective motives.** Sport evokes emotions, and the search for certain emotions is very frequently a deep-rooted motive. Certain sports are associated with strong feelings such as passion, fear, and the like; in others the emotions are less pronounced—attraction or pleasure, for example. An important step in categorising and measuring emotions in the consumption experience is due to Richins' (1997) research outcomes. Her Consumption Emotion Set identifies a range of 17 emotions: anger, discontent, worry, sadness, fear, shame, envy, loneliness, romantic love, love, peacefulness, contentment, optimism, joy, excitement, surprise, and others (guilty, proud, eager, and relieved). Sponsorship brings emotions that provoke goodwill and a positive attitude towards the sponsor's brand.

Attitude

Attitude is an explanatory variable that is essential to the consumer's decision-making process. The best-known definition is that by Fishbein and Ajzen (1975), for whom attitude is a "predisposition that has been learned in order to respond, coherently, and either favourably or unfavourably to a given object". Attitude thus expresses a state that predisposes a consumer to a type of behaviour when faced with the attributes of an object whose purpose is to satisfy physical, social or psychological needs. This corresponds to the concept by Hustad and Pessemier (1974), who consider that attitudes define individuals' approach to the persons and objects surrounding them. Constituted of beliefs, opinions, values, and preferences on the part of an individual as regards others and the environment, attitudes make it possible to foresee the person's behaviour to the extent that they reveal a predisposition regarding objects and other people. The basic idea is thus that all attitudes on the part of an individual, taken together, will reflect that person's various types of behaviour because they occur based on pre-existing dispositions.

This concept can also be applied easily to consumer behaviour. Here, attitude is defined as the consumer's positive or negative approach to a product or a brand (Assael, 1998). Nevertheless, certain authors understand this concept in a more narrow way, establishing a precise relation between it and the needs with which it is associated. Howard (1989) thus defines attitude to a brand as "the degree of satisfying the needs that the consumer considers this brand can bring him". Assael (1998) adopts a comparable position when he characterises attitude as "the evaluation by the consumer of the capacity of different brands or products to satisfy his needs". This second group of definitions underlines the contingent character of attitude. It also situates attitude in relation to the larger notion of image. According to Howard (1989) an image is a whole that consists of recognition of the brand and in particular of the category of products to which it belongs in the mind of the consumer; the consumer's attitude; and the confidence that the consumer attaches to his evaluation of this brand.

However, whatever the definition they use, all authors recognise that attitude is of central importance in the consumer's decision-making process. These researchers consider attitude a good means of predicting behaviour and thus of interest, but also a means of identifying the mechanisms that govern how attitude is formed. Influencing the behaviour of the consumer in a direction that is favourable to the brand or product usually means modifying the person's attitude towards it. Attitude towards an object can be assessed with a semantic scale (see figure 2.1).

Attitude is not, however, something with a single dimension. Rosenberg and Hovland (1960) present attitude as a psychological construct with three components: cognitive, affective, and behavioural. The definitions of attitude to which we have referred mainly involve the affective component, which corresponds to emotional reactions towards an object. The personal evaluation brought about by the affective component is extremely important since, as McGuire (1969) states, the cognitive and cona-

tive components vary. Thus, the more positive the evaluation is, the more there will be awareness of a problem and development of a major cognitive component regarding it. Similarly, the higher the affective component, the more this will serve as encouragement to take action.

The cognitive component of attitude is a psychological construct corresponding to the perception and the information that a person attributes to an object (such as table tennis). The content of this component is difficult to pinpoint given the diversity of the information base on which it can be structured. We nevertheless see that the beliefs that unite all the information concerning a social object or its environment can be classified into two categories. The first unites what we can call informative beliefs concerning the tangible attributes of the product. This conception is expressed in multi-attribute models, of which the best known is doubtless the compensatory model by Fishbein and Ajzen (1975). The second category refers to more subjective beliefs concerning the object. This corresponds to the approach by Kapferer (1988), which assimilates the image used in advertising with the cognitive structure of the attitude towards the brand. Whatever it is, this component refers to the relation between motives, criteria for choice, and the comprehension of the brand.

The conative component represents the predisposition to action concerning the object to which the attitude applies. The type of behaviour adopted results in the intensity of this component. The intention to purchase is directly related to this component. In fact, the intention to purchase corresponds to the disposition of a person who states that he or she is or is not in favour of purchasing goods or services. The conative attitude component

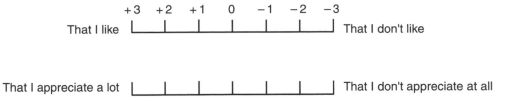

Figure 2.1 Attitude towards a sport can be defined by using a semantic scale.

can be assessed with a scale such as that shown in figure 2.2.

There are close relations among the components of attitude. The affective component was long considered the most important element of attitude and in particular the main decisive factor of behaviour. However, research has revealed the superiority of the multidimensional approach to attitude, notably in terms of the capacity to predict purchasing behaviour (Woodside, Clokey, and Combes, 1974).

Involvement

The concept of involvement has taken on considerable importance within the theory of consumer behaviour. Notably this concept has made it possible to re-envisage the effect of various stimuli on consumer behaviour, and in particular in the decision-making process adopted by the consumer depending on various levels of involvement (Kapferer and Laurent, 1985). Among the most frequently encountered definitions we shall retain that by Rothschild (1984), for whom "involvement is a state of motivation, interest or awareness. It is created by a specific object or a specific situation. It leads to types of behaviour, certain forms of searching for a product, information handling and decision making. ... This state exists within a process governed by external variables, the situation, the product, communication, and by internal variations to the subject and its fundamental values".

This definition leads us to consider involvement as a variable that characterises the relation between the consumer and products or situations (or both). It determines the degree of energy allocated to a series of tasks concerning certain products or situations that appear to be more or less central. For this reason, Kapferer and Laurent (1985) understand involvement as a motivational variable that makes it possible to grasp psychological states that rationality alone cannot explain.

Most actors have revealed the multidimensional character of involvement. After analysis of the various theoretical approaches concerning this concept, we note that they use a limited number of components that can be grouped into five categories: interest in the category of the product, the pleasure obtained from the product, and the capacity of the product to express status or personality, plus two aspects related to the perceived risk (Kapferer and Laurent, 1985).

- The personal interest in a category of products, its significance, and its importance. Practising sport organises the life of certain persons even though it is only a complement.

- The hedonist value, the emotional impact, the product's capacity to procure pleasure, sensations. Sport brings pleasure on both an individual level (for the player scoring a goal) and on a collective level (for other members of the team and the spectators).

Question: Choose one of the proposals below concerning Beach Volleyball World Tour

Only one response is possible

☐ 1. I shall certainly not attend a BVWT event this season.

☐ 2. I shall probably not attend a BVWT event this season.

☐ 3. It is possible that I shall not attend a BVWT event this season.

☐ 4. I do not know whether I shall attend a BVWT event this season.

☐ 5. It is possible that I shall attend a BVWT event this season.

☐ 6. I shall probably attend a BVWT event this season.

☐ 7. I shall certainly attend a BVWT event this season.

Figure 2.2 Measuring the conative component of attitude to a sport.[2]

[2] The direct method is simple to use. You can reduce the number of proposals to five by deleting the statements including the term "possible".

- The value of the sign attributed by the consumer to the product, its purchase, and its consumption. Like all types of consumption, sport has a utility value (functional benefits) and a sign value (symbolic and social benefits). Does the choice of a sport, a team, or an event reflect a certain image of the person who practises, supports, or attends? Thus, football club Olympic Marseille constitutes an important element for the identity of inhabitants of the South of France.

- The subjective probability of making a mistake at the moment of purchase. Is there a strong risk of making the wrong choice?

- The perceived importance of the negative consequences of making the wrong choice when buying a product or a service. If an error takes place, what is the degree of gravity of the negative consequences?

EXHIBIT 2.2 MEASURING INVOLVEMENT

Here, it is a question of formulating questions relating to each dimension of commitment. Table 2.1 presents some examples, linked to a six-point evaluation scale: 1. Absolutely disagree; 2. Disagree; 3. Don't really agree; 4. Agree a little; 5. Agree; 6. Absolutely agree.

It is worthwhile asking two or three questions per dimension in order to better evaluate them. The average responses for each dimension are then calculated (figure 2.3).

Data presented on the graph show that beach volleyball fans who attended and didn't attend an event have a different involvement profile. Subscribed supporters have higher averages regarding interest and pleasure and lower ones regarding the two dimensions linked to risk.

Table 2.1 Examples of Questions Relating to the Five Dimensions of Involvement

Dimension	Sample question	Evaluation scale					
Interest, importance	BVB is very important for me.	1	2	3	4	5	6
Pleasure	For me, BVB equals pleasure.	1	2	3	4	5	6
Identification, sign	In a way, BVB expresses someone's personality.	1	2	3	4	5	6
Probability of making mistake when purchasing	It's always hard to choose a BVB event to attend.	1	2	3	4	5	6
Gravity of the risk	It's very annoying to attend to a BVB event if it isn't right for you.	1	2	3	4	5	6

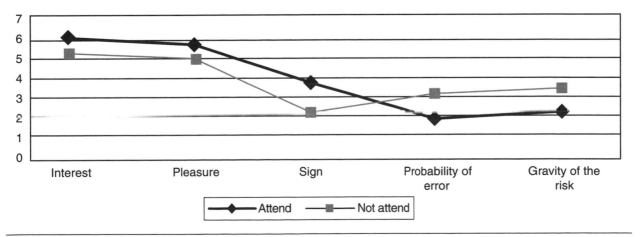

Figure 2.3 Beach volleyball fans' involvement profile.

Brand Loyalty

In the previous chapter we stressed that loyalty is an OSO brand equity component. Sport organisations are seeking to create loyalty among their members, partners, sponsors, and so on from a defensive point of view. This does not, however, exclude offensive action that seeks to derive benefit from the fact that the marketing target lacks loyalty during leisure time. If we consider the frequency of the "purchases", we can pinpoint two situations:

1. Situations implying a long-term commitment. This is the case of subscribed members and certain sponsors who have involvement for at least one year.

2. Repeated purchases during the course of a year. This is the case of spectators and sponsors who have involvement for a single operation.

In this context, loyalty is an extremely important concept that must be understood from a psychological point of view and that must be managed from a strategic point of view.

In the area of marketing, the notion of loyalty has been the subject of a very large number of studies that have made it possible to gain a better understanding of this concept. According to Engel, Kollat, and Blackwell (1973), "Loyalty is the attitudinal and behavioural response of a consumer expressing his preference, stable over time, for one (or several) brand(s) in a given category of products". It is thus a question of the consumer's tendency to purchase, regularly, one and the same brand in a specific category of products, supported by a favourable and lasting attitude towards this brand. According to Jacoby (1971), "Loyalty to the brand is the biased behavioural response (purchase), expressed over time, by decision-making units toward one (or several) alternative brand(s) or a group of brands, and depending on a psychological process (decision and evaluation)". From these definitions, it is clear that loyalty includes the following:

- A (favourable) attitudinal dimension that corresponds to the affective dimension of attitude that we have presented
- A dimension linked to the choice between various alternatives
- A behavioural dimension (repeated purchase)

Jacoby's definition has the advantage of combining the behaviourist approach with the determinist one; these were long opposed with respect to the nature of loyalty. The behaviourist school, in fact, considers loyalty to be simply a type of purchasing behaviour. The loyal consumer is the one who systematically buys the same brand. The determinist (or attitudinal) perspective is interested in the psychological antecedents of purchasing behaviour. A loyal consumer shows a stable preference towards the brand. The intersection of the two approaches has given rise to the composite approach (see figure 2.4). This considers that loyalty has a behavioural component (renewed purchase) that is the result of a psychological process (attitudinal component). A loyal consumer regularly purchases the same brand and shows a stable preference to it.

In the composite approach, it is therefore necessary to measure the attitude towards the sport organisation with the help of a semantic scale of the type "I like versus I don't like", or "I

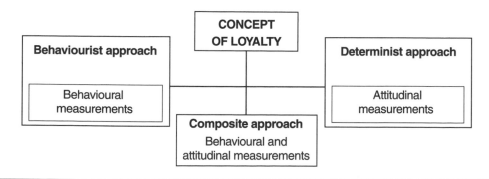

Figure 2.4 The three main approaches to loyalty.

prefer or don't prefer". Concerning behavioural measurement, we recommend using measurement by sequence of purchase. This type of measurement is based on the chronological order of purchases and on the analysis of successive sequences of purchases on the part of consumers.

EXHIBIT 2.3 EVALUATING LOYALTY LEVEL BASED ON SEQUENCES OF PURCHASES

Brown (1952), who was one of the first authors to propose a measurement of loyalty according to this approach, considers loyalty to be "a deliberate decision to concentrate purchasing on a single brand because of its real or imagined superiority". From analysis of purchasing histories, Brown isolates four main types of brand loyalty (see table 2.2):

- Exclusive loyalty (a single, same brand purchased)
- Divided loyalty (systematic, regular purchase, alternating between two brands)
- Unstable loyalty (two sequences of exclusive loyalty)
- Disloyalty (successive purchases of different brands)

Table 2.2 **The Four Types of Brand Loyalty**

Purchases	1	2	3	4	5	6
Exclusive loyalty	A	A	A	A	A	A
Divided loyalty	A	A	A	B	A	B
Unstable loyalty	A	A	A	C	B	B
Disloyalty	A	B	C	D	E	F

Note: A, B, C, D, E, and F are sport events.

Segmentation of Consumers Based on Involvement and Loyalty

While one is examining the variables that can affect the consumer's behaviour, one should take into account another factor that is capable of affecting behaviour and escaping the rational aspect of making a purchase: emotions. Affective reactions have in fact recently been considered by several authors as fundamental to the decision-making process. We develop this point within the framework of the experiential approach.

Combining the variables of loyalty and involvement makes it possible to reveal a typology of consumers. Figure 2.5 permits the definition of four categories.

Considering beach volleyball club members, we will place members in four sectors as follows:

- Sector 1. Members who are strongly committed but by no means loyal. They do not hesitate to change clubs if they are not satisfied.
- Sector 2. Members who are loyal and committed. They are satisfied in relation to their major expectations or have a strong socio-affective link with the club.
- Sector 3. Members who are neither very committed nor loyal. They would like to try out a sport activity with their friends.
- Sector 4. Members who are loyal yet not very committed. The reasons for their loyalty can lie in a family tradition of membership.

These variables also influence the member's decision-making process. Later on we present a typology.

Environmental Influences

Environmental influences are variables other than individual psychological and cognitive factors that have an influence on the behaviour of the consumer in the marketplace. Because individuals are interacting in a social

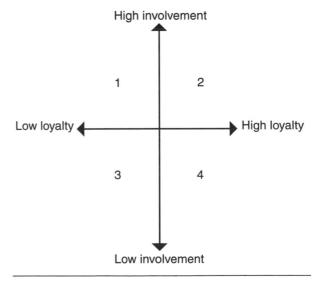

Figure 2.5 Segmentation based on the level of loyalty and the level of involvement.

environment, some major social influences exist. We develop two main factors: reference groups and culture.

Reference Groups

A reference group is a group of people or an organisation that an individual respects, identifies with, or aspires to join—for example, membership or associative groups. The group serves as a reference point for the individual in forming his or her beliefs, attitudes, and behaviour.

A membership group is a group of individuals within which the individual is psychologically and formally a member. A sport club and a group of fans are examples of membership groups. In these groups the individual has direct, face-to-face psychological relations and interdependence with other members. A person can aspire to belong to a group. In this case, the group is an aspiration group. If the person has a negative attitude, the group is considered a disclaimant group.

Assael (1998) segments reference groups considering two variables: formal versus informal and primary versus secondary. If a person has regular contact with group members, the group is a primary group; if those contacts are less frequent, the group is a secondary group. Assael underlines the existence of two types of aspiration groups considering the contact with group members. If individuals intend to join, the group is an anticipatory aspiration group. If this is not the case, the group is a symbolic aspiration group.

Sport consumption is related to all these types of groups. From an institutional point of view, a sport organisation can be a membership group or a nonmembership group. Sport is a major socialisation medium. It provides roles—for example, president, coach, athlete, volunteer—bringing norms, values, and a social position or status to individuals. It carries values and norms, for example standards of conduct established by the group.

These groups have a power related to their influence on individuals. Sport influence groups can have power due to their expertise. They can be a source of an individual's identification, and their rewards can be highly appreciated. Reference groups can exert three types of influence:

- Informational influence. A group can exert this type of influence because it is a credible source of information and expertise.
- Comparative influence. This type of influence occurs when individuals relate their values, attitudes, and lifestyle to a group they agree or don't agree with. Individuals look for consistency and enhance their self-concept by associating with groups that will provide reinforcement and ego gratification.
- Normative influence refers to the influence exerted on an individual by a reference group to conform to its norms. It can have an opposite effect when the person rejects conformity.

Research on sport socialisation (see Brustad, 1992 for a review) has focused on how individuals

- learn skills, values, attitudes, norms, and knowledge on sport roles through direct and indirect interaction with social systems; and
- are attracted to sport (socialisation into sport), the consequences of sport involvement (socialisation through sport), and also the factors that facilitate sport withdrawal (socialisation out of sport).

The power of socialisation relates to the group influence on individuals. This can be a result of expertise (coach), the power of identification (team fans), or reward (sport trophies and celebrations).

Opinion Leaders

Reference groups are not the only ones to consider. Some individuals have a personal influence on other members' attitudes, opinions, and behaviour. The most influential people are termed opinion leaders, the ones to whom others turn for advice and information. Sport generates many kinds of opinion leaders, among them coaches and top athletes. Sport celebrities represent a member of a group the consumer admires at a distance. Marketers use sport celebrities as spokespersons to try to mirror group influence. There are some some good examples on the Web sites of Real Madrid (www.realmadrid.com); Adidas, Real Madrid official supplier, (www.adidas.com/); and Zinedine Zidane, one of the club's top players (www.zidane.fr)

Culture

A culture is a system of shared beliefs, values, customs, behaviours, and artefacts that the members of society use to cope with their world and with one another, and that are transmitted from generation to generation through learning. It is the broadest environmental factor affecting consumer behaviour. Through education, each person assimilates the value system characteristic of his or her culture. This is the result of efforts accepted by society for the purpose of fitting in with the environment. In this way the consumer behaviour of a European, an Asian, and an American is subject to different cultural influences.

In the first chapter we defined values as an enduring prescriptive or proscriptive belief that a specific end state of existence or specific mode of conduct is preferable to an opposite end state or mode of conduct for living one's life. Values refer both to individuals and to groups. At the individual level, values are internalised. At a group level, values are scripts or cultural ideals held in common by members of a group—the group ideals. Differences in these cultural ideals, especially those with a moral component, determine and distinguish different social systems. Values are internalised, and individuals take on values as part of socialisation into membership groups, reference groups, and society. They are relatively fixed over time and generate principles guiding action. Culture not only influences consumer behaviour but also reflects it.

Rokeach (1973) developed the Rokeach Value Survey, designed to measure two sets of values (table 2.3). The first is composed of 18 items. The second is composed of 18 instrumental values, or preferable modes of behaviour. In other words, instrumental values are end states of existence that are preferred over other end states, such as a comfortable life, a sense of accomplishment, a world of peace, and racial equality. Terminal values, for example peace and freedom, are goals for the whole society and individuals. This conceptualisation links individual values and cultural values.

Table 2.3 **The Rokeach Value Survey (1973)**

Terminal value	Instrumental value
A comfortable life	Ambitious
A sense of accomplishment	Broadminded
A world at peace	Capable
A world of beauty	Cheerful
An exciting life	Clean
Equality	Courageous
Family security	Forgiving
Freedom	Helpful
Happiness	Honest
Inner harmony	Imaginative
Mature love	Independent
National security	Intellectual
Pleasure	Logical
Salvation	Loving
Self-respect	Obedient
Social recognition	Polite
True friendship	Responsible

Each culture has a specific set of socially acquired values that that society accepts as a whole. These values are under a double influence: globalisation and differentiation. Globalisation is a social change, increasing connections among society. It can apply to many social, cultural, commercial, and economic activities. From a cultural point of view, globalisation means closer contact between different parts of the world, with increasing possibilities of personal exchange and mutual understanding, sharing of values, and common social representations. Olympism has a strong social impact. It is a multicultural phenomenon aiming at developing universal values and preserving national identities. Its goal is to "place sport everywhere at the service of the harmonious development of humankind, with a view to encouraging the establishment of a peaceful society concerned with the preservation of human dignity. Blending sport with culture and education, Olympism seeks to create a way of life based on the joy found in effort, the educational value of good example and respect for universal fundamental ethical principles" (Rogge, 2004). The International Olympic Committee (IOC) launched a new rendition of its global promotional campaign, "Celebrate Humanity", to be shown in the lead-up to the Athens 2004 Olympic Games. The 2004 Celebrate Humanity campaign highlighted the Olympic values of hope, dreams and inspiration, joy in effort, friendship, and fair play, as told through emotive narratives by internationally recognised spokespeople.

Differentiation is related to the existence of subcultures. A subculture is a set of people with distinct behaviour and beliefs within a larger culture. The essence of a subculture, which distinguishes it from a mere social grouping, is awareness of style and differences in values and lifestyle. A culture often contains numerous subcultures. Subcultures incorporate large parts of their mother cultures, but in specific instances they may differ radically. Some subcultures achieve such a status that they acquire a name of their own. In this respect, sport can be related to subcultures based on specific values. Fun sports provide a positive experience for people who want to share certain values such as hedonism, exciting life, friendship, and group belonging. There are other subcultures based on factors like age, geography, religion, and ethnicity.

Analysing the Decision-Making Process

It is now necessary to go beyond the simple identification of the variables influencing the sport consumer. It is necessary to penetrate into the consumer "black box" that is the process of decision. We have stressed that from a marketing point of view, this conveys two types of decisions. The first relates to loyalty; the second concerns the first purchase in a competitive environment. Different decision-making processes have been identified, and we present in the first instance their dynamics. Secondly we present a typology of this process, allowing for categorisation.

Decision-Making Process Dynamic

Sport consumers' and sponsors' decision-making processes vary depending on a number of factors. From a generic point of view, a decision-making process like this can be described as having five different stages (see figure 2.6).

Let's take an example in the sponsorship sector.

1. A company is developing its business in a foreign market. The marketing strategist wants to increase the brand awareness and to create a positive attitude towards the brand. The target is a male from 16 to 65 years old.

2. The company is looking for communication opportunities in order to achieve these objectives.

3. Companies get various sponsorship proposals from clubs, top athletes, and events. They assess the relevance of each proposal.

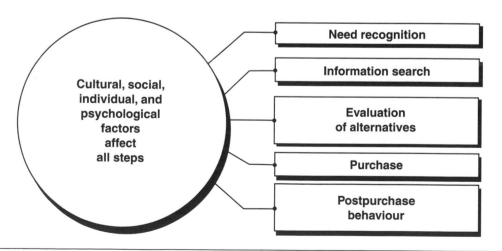

Figure 2.6 Five steps of the consumer decision-making process.

4. They decide to be the naming rights sponsor of the national soccer cup.

5. After this event they assess the return on investment in order to maintain this sponsorship programme or to develop alternative communications strategies.

Researchers have demonstrated that this process is not linear. The models expressing the decision-making process stressed the variables to consider and the relationships between them, for example involvement, attitude, expectations, and satisfaction. Although some details vary, all the models are organised on the basis of a series of four phases: marketing stimuli, perception, information analysis, and response. The illustrative model is presented in figure 2.7.

Next we present each phase of decision making in more detail by defining the basic concepts to consider and their relationships.

1. Stimulation Phase The stimulation phase concerns the environment in which the sport consumer is situated. The consumer is stimulated by offers to satisfy different types of motives, for example functional, symbolic,

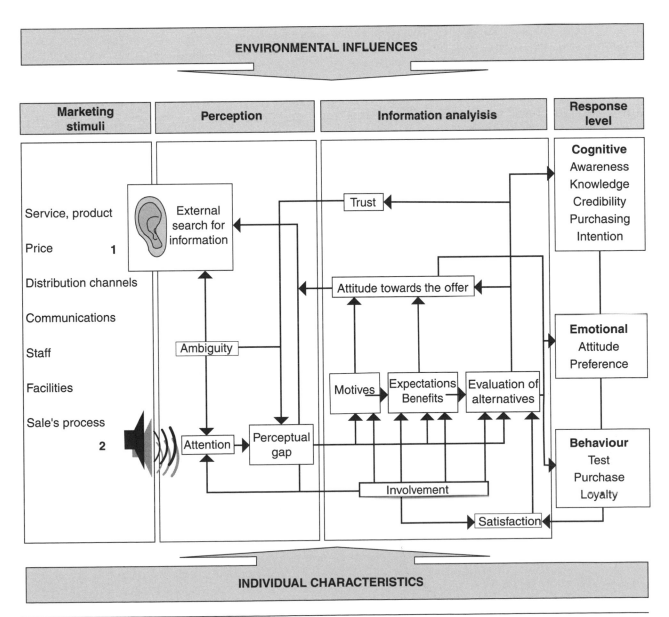

Figure 2.7 An illustrative model of the consumer decision-making process (Ferrand and Nardi, in press).

affective, social, and cultural. Marketing action is differentiated in order to conceive an offer to a specific segment of consumers considering its motives.

It is important to understand that marketing action is a stimulus. It is possible to stimulate the individuals belonging to the target group using variables such as service or product (or both), price, communications, sales process, and OSO staff and facilities. Olympic sport organisations offer services aimed at fulfilling the target audience's expectations, within a context that is defensive, or offensive, or both. Strategies concern price, communication, and distribution. There are two situations:

1. The target is looking for information in order to fulfil his or her expectations, and it is easy to stimulate the target with the marketing action. For example, parents who have just moved house and who wish their child to join a sport club will be much more attentive, during the month of September, to information from publicity in their mailboxes, advice from teachers, articles in the press, and so on.

2. The target is not looking for information, possibly because the person has no precise needs or because the individual is confident enough about his or her knowledge in order to make a decision. In this case, marketing action is more challenging.

2. Phase of Perception and of Handling Information   We live in a world in which offers are abundant and we are assailed by a vast variety of messages. The phase of perception and of handling information is situated in this context. Getting attention and being perceived without ambiguity is the challenge.

This phase can be a source of conflict if the information is contradictory—for example, in the case in which a club has a good reputation but the coach does not seem very accessible or communicative during a visit.

3. Phase of Information Analysis and Apprenticeship   The phase relating to the perceptual construct interacts with that relating to the apprenticeship construct. Earlier we stressed the importance of motives and expectations that lead to criteria for choice. The consumer "understands" sport brand offers in the marketplace. In fact, if parents consider all the volleyball clubs that exist in the town where they live, they will perceive them via their own personal "filter". A club has a brand designating services offered in the marketplace in a distinctive manner. Previous experience is likely to intervene in a decisive way if the person has already experienced the club's services. His or her level of satisfaction[3] will have a direct influence on his or her comprehension of the brand.

Whatever the service proposed and whatever the brand associated with it, this must satisfy the motives, expectations, and criteria for choice more effectively than the competition can. These motives can be extremely clear and can be indicated during an individual or group discussion.

• Why do you practise beach volleyball? (Because it is fascinating, interesting, fun, fast; develops strategies; is technically complex; requires mental and physical concentration; is a combination of mental, technical, and physical qualities.)

• What services should a club offer? It is then necessary to determine the level of importance of these motives based on a questionnaire in which the person responding is invited to indicate the importance he or she attributes to each expectation regarding the service. A decisive expectation will be directly linked to the person's choice or to his or her preference of a club or the services it offers.

EXHIBIT 2.4 MERCHANDISE PRODUCTS OF A VOLLEYBALL CLUB

The next example concerns clothing merchandise products. Each supporter was asked to rate the importance of each attribute on a scale of 1 to 5 using a "smiling face". The results are listed in table 2.4.

---

[3] At a later stage, we shall develop this concept in the section devoted to management of the quality of services and to satisfaction. At this point, we present an evaluation method along with the appropriate tools.

Table 2.4 **Characteristics That Should Distinguish Clothing Related to a Volleyball Club**

Attributes	Means
Should be available in the club colours	4.60
Should be available in all sizes	4.62
The club logo should be visible	4.55
The fabric should be good quality	4.35
Trendy	4.28
Resistant	4.18
Should bear the club name	4.12
Should bear players' names	3.98
There should be products for women	3.58
Should be associated with a major brand name	3.34
Should be elegant	3.23
Should be made by Nike (the sponsor)	3.19

4. Decision Phase   At the end of this process, there are three levels of response:

- The cognitive level refers to awareness, knowledge of the OSO offer, and credibility.
- The emotional level refers to the connection with affective attitude and preference.
- Behavioural outcomes are exemplified by, for example, testing the offer, purchasing for the first time, or being loyal.

Typology of the Consumer's Decision-Making Process

Depending on the level of involvement and on the consequences of making a wrong decision, the complexity of this process can range from careful analysis to pure impulse. While an impulse buy, such as purchase of a packet of chewing gum, can take place instantaneously, complex purchases mostly stretch over a long period of time. This buying process is an iterative process, in which people collect information from different sources and repeatedly return to reevaluate and compare the information they have found. Despite the large diversity of circumstances, those processes can fit into a typology. Assael (1998) built a typology based on two dimensions: the extent of decision making and the degree of involvement in the purchase.

Involvement refers to the individual's motivation state (presented previously). There are high-involvement purchase dimensions, for example signing a sponsorship deal as a main partner for a world event, and low-involvement ones like renewal of a season ticket by an Arsenal fan after the team has won the championship. The extent of the decision making considers the information search and evaluation of brand alternatives. It can be extensive or limited. Here we characterise these decision-making processes as complex decision making, limited decision making, dissonance-reducing decision making, and routine.

Complex Decision Making   In the process of complex decision making, consumers seek a large quantity of information on both an internal level (linked to their experience) and an external one (documentation, experts, publicity, etc.). They are thus seeking to make the purchase that is most in line with their expectations. These latter may evolve depending on the search for external information. Potential conflicts thus exist among the sources of information. The consumer evaluates all the possible alternatives.

The consumer is strongly involved and perceives the major differences between brands and what is offered. In this process, the consumer's decision will be based on evaluating each alternative depending on its characteristics (attributes) as compared with the person's expectations. This process falls within the framework of the multi-attribute models that we have presented.

The ideal offer rarely exists. In this context, the formation of preferences takes place with the help of the compensatory norm in which an interesting characteristic can compensate for another, less appealing one. Fishbein's model presents this process regulated by the compensatory norm in a simple way.

Typical situations for complex decision making in sport include the following:

- Sponsors intending to make an important first deal with an OSO
- Dissatisfied club members highly involved and looking for a change

Limited Decision Making In a low-involvement situation, the decision-making process leads the consumer to choose rapidly, particularly since the perceived risk is low. The search for information is limited, and the choice will be guided by a simple reason: brand already purchased, lower price, proximity, availability. Typical situations for complex decision making in sport include these:

- Satisfied sponsors intending to renew their deal
- Satisfied club members who are highly involved

Dissonance-Reducing Decision Making This process occurs when consumers are highly involved (notably if the perceived risk is high), but see little difference among offers. Typical situations for complex decision making in sport are the following:

- Sponsors intending to make an important first deal with an OSO
- Satisfied club members who are highly involved

Habitual Decision Making and Inertia Another form of decision making concerns all decisions to purchase that are taken out of habit, without particular reflection, either for physical reasons or because of the impossibility of choosing (due to either conscious loyalty to a brand or inertia). In habitual decision making, the consumer has integrated the reasons for his or her choice. Inertia (or unconscious loyalty) is due to the fact that the consumer does not bother about this decision.

These processes are carried out within a context of low involvement and little significant difference between alternatives. The consumer systematically selects the same brand again out of habit. Habitual decision making and inertia can tire the consumer and bring about the desire to change. The following are typical situations for complex decision making in sport:

- Some sport club honorary members
- Satisfied club members with low involvement

Variety-Seeking Buying Behaviour When low-involved consumers perceive differences between alternatives, they can look for a change. It is difficult to deal with these individuals because they are satisfied and you cannot do much about it. They are considered switchers. It should be noted that the consumer can change his or her decision-making process depending on experience and familiarity with the product. Usually, the consumer evolves from complex decision making to routine resolution.

2.2 Managing the Target Audience Experience

The consumer's decision-making process as presented makes it possible to take into account a rational person seeking to find the best price/performance ratio. This is not always the case. The experiential flow (Holbrook and Hirschman, 1982) is intended to explain the consumer's purchasing behaviour based on sensations, emotions, and shared feelings linked to an individual or collective experience. This approach makes it possible to take into account the emotional and symbolic impact of a collective experience on certain purchasing situations. There are many examples of this within sport. The supporters of a football club continue to come to matches even when the club loses them all. Members of a tennis club remain loyal even though the service proposed is inferior to and more expensive than that of the competition. In this section we first summarise the key principles of traditional marketing. Secondly we develop the experiential approach. This approach is in line with the sport experience, and we will propose an operational framework in order to provide the right experience for OSO target audiences.

From Traditional to Experiential Marketing

The experiential flow (Holbrook and Hirschman, 1982) is intended to explain the consumer's behaviour on the basis of sensations, emotions, and feelings arising from an experience. This approach integrates the traditional marketing approach that favours the rational side of the consumer. It aims to produce the conditions necessary in order that the experience desired by consumers using the service will emerge. This strategy is widely used. For example, Microsoft Windows XP is a system intended to provide us with the socio-emotional experience we desire in parallel to its performance and reliability. Sport is the favoured area for applying this strategy, since it includes and goes beyond the emotional impact of a collective experience within the context of sport entertainment because of its symbolic significance.

Characteristics of Traditional Marketing

The traditional conception of marketing considers the consumer to be basically rational. The multi-attribute models express the decision-making mechanism. Numerous applications of this model have been used and have made it possible to establish its explanatory capacity in situations of extensive resolution (purchase of an apartment, a car, etc.). These consumer decisions demand a major investment on the part of the individual in terms of time and cognitive activity in order to seek out a considerable quantity of information. Applied to the area of sport, this approach presents the following characteristics:

- It focuses on rational functional motives and attributes. This leads to favouring technical elements of the service (competence of the coach, sport facilities, etc.).

- The competition is evaluated in the same product category. A sport is thus competing with another sport, and the clubs within the same federation are also competing against each other.

- The brand is seen to be a semantic element for the distinctive designation of the products and services offered on the market by the sport organisation. This means developing awareness of the brand and positioning its image based on functional benefits (athletics means developing physical qualities, coordination, etc.).

This is an operational framework for professional consumers as sponsors. Depending on their level of involvement, perception of differences between offers, and perceived risk, they will use a complex or dissonance-reducing decision-making process. We develop a strategic analysis in the chapter focusing on sponsorship.

The Characteristics of Experiential Marketing

Experiential marketing centres on the experiences of consumers. These experiences are private or social events that take place in response to certain stimuli. This type of marketing implicates the person as a whole and provokes emotions. Sport as a form of entertainment or a "show" is an environment in which it is likely that experience will emerge. Emotion is the essence of the events, and according to Maffesoli (1988), "Shared emotion . . . comes from the fact of taking part or corresponds—in the strong and perhaps mystical sense of the term—to a common ethos. Thus, that which is favoured is less what each will subscribe to voluntarily (contractual and mechanical perspective) than that which is an emotion common to all (sensitive and organic perspective)". This means that this is a fundamental mechanism through which the sport event produces an experience of identification within what could be termed "affectual communities". Moreover, ethnological analysis regarding the mass enthusiasm for the football clubs of Marseilles and Turin and their matches, carried out by Bromberger, Hayot, and Mariottini (1987), reveals and discriminates the relations between the symbolic and affective aspects. The mobilisation of the affective aspect in these communities takes place within specific, symbolic places.

The experiential approach integrates the traditional approach in considering consumers as both rational and emotional. This means they can make rational choices as regards jogging in order to keep in shape, for instance, and focus more on their emotions when it comes to choosing a ski resort.

EXHIBIT 2.5 DECISIVE FACTORS FOR SATISFYING REGISTERED FOOTBALL SUPPORTERS

Research carried out by Beccarini (2001) on factors that determine the loyalty of Olympic Lyonnais Football Club season ticket owners showed that the financial advantages constituted an influence that was double that of the image dimension leading to categorisation of the club as a "major club".

Table 2.5 reveals the relations between the three variables representing the match attributes, the attribute of being a subscribed supporter, and the image. This in turn reveals the structure of the model by showing how the evaluation made by the supporter consists of experiences and emotions that are interlinked in order to form a specific process.

On a more detailed level (table 2.6), we note that the two variables that exert a direct influence on satisfaction are influenced by other variables. More precisely, the variable represented by the image of a major club is influenced by two factors: the performance of the team (subscription attributes) and pleasure in the show aspect (match attributes). The first has a cognitive-dominant effect; the second, an affective one. It is, in fact, fairly logical for the image of a major club to be linked to the perception of the "show", that is, the football match (performance of the team, good players recruited, good season), and by the socio-emotional situation (sharing the atmosphere, celebration, pleasure). The strong link between the image of a major club and the team's performance is in line with the positive influence of technical interest on team performance. Interest in the show aspect positively influences the other cognitive factors: interest in the team when it performs well, seeing goals scored, seeing the other team. The image of a major club in turn influences the factor expressing the financial advantages (subscription attributes). Consequently, a component that links the cognitive and affective aspects, plus one that is completely emotional, partly justifies the influence of the factor associated with the financial advantages (completely cognitive) of the satisfaction. Analysis of these causality chains thus expresses a logic. The value of the show in terms of price is linked to its quality. The price/quality ratio represents the key to analysing this aspect.

These data enable us to gain a better understanding of this experience; through such understanding the club can manage its relation with supporters who have taken out a subscription. Consumption is a holistic experience and should not be considered only in terms of football, athletics, or tennis. As a marketer, you must supply the environment, service, and organisation that make it possible for the experience desired by the consumer to emerge.

Initially, therefore, you must define the type of experience that you wish to make available to your consumers. For this, we shall use the system presented by Schmitt (1999), which concerns sensations, feelings, thoughts, communication aiming to tell a story, and action.

On a sensorial level, spectators listen, see, and have physical contact with the other spectators. Regarding feelings, it is necessary for them to feel

Table 2.5 **Direct Effects on Satisfaction**

Dimension	Dominant	Influence	Standardised parameters (from 0 to 1)
Financial advantages	Cognitive	Positive	0.47
Image of a major club	Cognitive/ Affective	Positive	0.22

Table 2.6 **Effects Between Variables Relating to Reasons for Subscribing, Image, and Attributes of the Match in Gerland (France)**

Dimensions that exert an influence	Dominant	Influence	Dimensions affected by the influence	Standardised parameters
Pleasure in the show aspect	Affective	Positive	Financial advantages	0.29
Performance by the team	Cognitive	Positive	Image of a major club	0.40
Pleasure in the show aspect	Affective	Positive	Image of a major club	0.28
Image of a major club	Cognitive/Affective	Positive	Financial advantages	0.31
Technical interest	Cognitive	Positive	Performance by the team	0.31

excitement, warmth, pleasure, and enthusiasm. For thought, it is a question of inviting supporters to make proposals aimed at improving their communication and their life with the club. Finally, regarding action, it is a question of permitting them to express and liberate themselves, giving an impetus to their lifestyle.

The question then is one of defining and planning the use of experience "suppliers". These are actions that you will carry out in order to create the environmental conditions that will make it possible for this experience to emerge. The main one concerns the basic service, which must aim to satisfy the subscribed members' most important expectations. It is here that experiential marketing integrates traditional marketing. Analysis of expectations on the part of supporters relating to watching a home football match reveals three dimensions:

- The most important concerns the festive atmosphere (being in the mood, having fun, taking part in a show and a celebration)
- The second relates to self-expression (letting loose, expressing one's dynamism, going out).
- The last refers to interest in sport (seeing goals being scored, seeing the team performing well, seeing the other team).

It is very important to note that the two most important components for subscribed supporters of this club concern the emotional dimensions. In order to satisfy them, the stadium must be prepared (be close to the field, provide good vision and sound, etc.) to organise and promote the show aspect (flags, hymns, music, singing, team's style of play, commentator, etc.). The sport component certainly depends on the sport results but also on the team's style of play and the personality of the players.

A certain number of peripheral elements must be associated with this basic service. Among these, we underline the importance of communication: This must be reactive. Subscribed supporters need to speak out, to express their feelings regarding the club. To give them this opportunity, you can use reply coupons in the press, a toll-free telephone number, games and competitions, articles that encourage subscribers to write in or call (on the condition that you organise yourself to provide responses to their comments), mail order, and so on. Direct marketing also favours reaction on the part of the prospect. It is important to stress that it is the feedback from the person who is there to provide responses that creates personalised contact. This reactive communication is often on a one-to-one basis. It is greatly facilitated by the use of new technologies, and establishes individual contact while reinforcing a special, personal link.

Peripheral events help make relations between supporters and the club "gel". According to Piquet (1985), an event is first and foremost a "strong social issue, a place where men and women get together in a sort of collective celebration in order to attend a sports or cultural type of entertainment. This is subjectively perceived as the possibility of achieving an exploit". Events constitute the basic activity of a football club. This activity can be expanded: For example, the Olympique Lyonnais club created the OL Tour, which included events, a competition, and a village where sponsors proposed promotional offers. By their presence and their advice, the players and coaches add dynamism to such events.

Generally speaking it is essential to involve the emblematic individuals in a club (its president, the star players, past stars) and the sponsors. These latter must be carefully selected. We shall develop this aspect in the chapter devoted to sponsoring. Sponsors are not just a source of financing; they also constitute one of the components of the club and must be anchored within its culture. It is thus wise to collaborate with sponsors that "fit" the club well, through setting up activities that permit the sponsor to work actively with the supporters by supplying a tangible advantage (public relations, test products, games and competitions, etc.).

All those who provide the possibility of experiences permit the club to activate its brand among its supporters during and outside the matches (one-to-one communication, peripheral events, public relations, special offers, derivative products, etc.). The brand must be a supplier of experience. It brings with it a lifestyle. It creates a relation with the club. For this reason, the identity (visual, sound, etc.) must be related to the experience in question.

How to Manage the OSO Targeted Audience Experience

According to the EX Group's CEM Framework™,[4] "When brands are seen as experience providers, equity is measured in their sensory

---

[4] www.exgroup.com

stimulation, emotional bonding, and lifestyle value. . . . To build and sustain a powerful brand, OSOs need to ensure an integrated customer experience that is delivered through communications, products, service, personnel, and every customer contact".

To conceive a strategy and implement the experiential marketing process we develop a four-step framework adapted from Schmitt (2004)—using strategic analysis to build the brand platform, choosing and designing the brand experience providers in relation to strategic experience modules, and managing the quality system (figure 2.8). We illustrate this process with the case of beach volleyball managed by FIVB.[5]

Strategic Analysis

This analysis focuses on the individuals who are already part of the OSO community or have been targeted for recruitment by the OSO.

Analysis of Customer's Experiential World
According to Cova and Roncaglio (1999), "tribal marketing" is a customised and interactive relationship with a targeted audience used to create a conviviality-stimulating system of values specific to a "tribe". The authors distinguish four

roles for people in the tribe corresponding to their position in this structure:

1. Members: They are invisible and countable. They belong to institutions, for example organisations.
2. Participants and spectators: They are visible and countable. They are occasional (events).
3. Sympathisers: They are invisible and difficult to catch. They share the same lifestyle (social trend and imaginary).
4. Individuals: They are invisible and difficult to catch. They are involved through an everyday practice (real-life experience).

In this context FIVB should analyse these social trends in order to identify modern "tribe" members with a lifestyle matching the beach volleyball lifestyle. Lifestyle is "different from the traditional status order it replaces and from modern structural divisions (such as class, gender and ethnicity) in at least two crucial respects. Firstly, it tends to indicate a purely 'cultural' pattern; it is made of signs, representations, media, and it is as mutable and understandable. Secondly, one can in theory

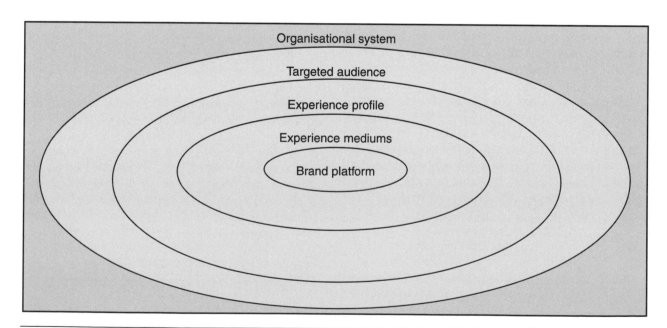

Figure 2.8 Experiential marketing layers.

[5] www.fivb.org

switch from one shop-window, TV channel, super-market shelf to another. The instability of the modern self is thus partly understood as an aspect of the instability of modern forms of social membership" (Slater, 1997). A *lifestyle* is the way a person (or a group) lives. This includes patterns of social relations, consumption, entertainment, and dress. A lifestyle typically also reflects an individual's attitudes, values, or world view. Having a specific "lifestyle" implies a conscious or unconscious choice between one set of behaviours and some other sets of behaviours.

Marketing consultants Popcorn and Marigold, in their best-selling book *Clinking,* attempt to predict what will happen next and what consumers will want. The beach volleyball lifestyle matches 6 out of 16 trends. These are presented in table 2.7.

This allows us to refer to the tendencies underlined earlier—research on emotional experience, creation of "community" in the modes of the tribes with their territory and their signs of recognition (they could be virtual)—in order to clarify the target of beach volleyball.

Competitor Analysis   It is important to survey the experiences offered by two types of competitors.

• Direct competitors of FIVB beach volleyball are sport organisations that manage sports associated with this lifestyle and these cultural trends. A few other beach team sports—beach soccer (www.beachsoccer.com), sand ball (www.sandball.com), and a major team sport like NBA basketball (www.nba.com)—should be considered.

• Indirect competitors are mainly concerts and online video games.

Self-Analysis   It is necessary to perform a diagnosis of the current situation taking into account OSO brand foundations, that is, heritage, vision, existing image, and current identity. We presented these concepts in the first chapter. The FIVB beach volleyball self-analysis is presented in table 2.8.

Constructing the OSO Brand Foundations

The brand foundations are communicated through verbal and visual imagery associated with the company and its brand. These foundations can be built through three elements: positioning, benefits, and theme.

Positioning   In the previous chapter we defined positioning as the part of the identity of the sport organisation that must be communicated actively to the various targets and that reveals a competitive advantage compared with the organisation's rivals. Al Ries and Jack Trout (1981) stressed the fact that "positioning is what you do to the mind of the prospect. That is, you position the product in the mind of the prospect".

In an experiential perspective one needs to specify what the OSO brand stands for and the core experience value promise related to it.

Table 2.7   Cultural Trends Matching FIVB Beach Volleyball

Trend	Characteristics
Clanning	People want to be part of, or to belong to, a social group. They feel safe, and it is reinforcing or providing social values, beliefs and lifestyle.
Fantasy adventure	In order to escape from life pressure, people are looking for safe and exciting entertainment. It could be through festive events, sport, travel, or the Internet.
Focus on pleasure	Modern society is focused on job achievement and those who are bringing more rules and regulations. People want to feel free and to get pleasure without guilt.
Anchoring	It is important to be aware of where you are from and where you are going to be. The past and the tradition allow people to reach back to their spiritual roots and provide the confidence in their capacity to manage the future.
Being alive	Being fit and healthy in order to improve your quality of life.

Table 2.8 FIVB and FIVB Beach Volleyball Self-Analysis

Heritage	Fun sport that first developed on the Californian and Brazilian beaches by players who wanted to have fun while playing volleyball on the beach in an outdoor environment with simple rules before reaching out.
Vision	Develop and establish the highest level of beach volleyball in every aspect of the game, event environment, participation, production, site, pleasure, sponsorship, and media support worldwide through the creation of a strong unique and differentiated brand. Main values to be conveyed are fun, excitement, pleasure, beauty, relaxation, fitness, friendliness, and musicality, but play is demanding and requires skill.
Existing image	An image of a fun, cool, trendy beach sport to play, participate in, and attend in the finest places and with the best athletes in the world.
Identity	The world top-quality brand in beach volleyball, associated with the finest environment, best organisation, and best players; highly prized and sanctioned by the governing body, the FIVB, providing quality service to all its stakeholders.

FIVB Beach Volleyball World Tour stands for "Share and experience the passion for an authentic fun beach sport in a unique combination of attributes".

Simply, FIVB Beach Volleyball World Tour stands for "the Best of Beach Volleyball".

Benefits Benefits—precisely what the positioning will provide to the customer—need to be specified. Specification is a promise to individuals and groups who have the given motives and expectations. The FIVB beach volleyball experience is directly related to certain benefits that the consumer will get. Earlier we stressed four categories of motives. When these are fulfilled by the consumption experience, the consumer gets related benefits—for example, cognitive, emotional, sociocultural, and psychological. We stress the fact that traditional marketing is aimed at providing cognitive benefits and that experiential marketing is focused on emotional and sociocultural benefits.

Cognitive Benefits Even if experiential marketing aims at creating emotions in order to satisfy the heart, the OSO should deliver cognitive benefits matching certain rational expectations, that is, safety, responsiveness, comfort.

For both players and spectators, FIVB beach volleyball provides the following benefits: major competitions, skills, fitness, physical beauty, entertainment, safety, comfort, and responsive service.

Rational benefits, when they are based on facts, are easily understood by the audience.

Furthermore they can provide the entry conditions to interest the target. Because they are based on facts, they can be easily copied or matched by competitors.

Emotional Benefits Richins (1997) views emotion as a "valenced affective reaction to perception of situations". Emotions are often accompanied by physiological and psychological states (feelings). Richins developed the Consumption Emotion Set (CES) to assess the range of emotions most frequently experienced in consumption situations. It covers 16 identifiable clusters comprising 43 descriptors (i.e., items): anger, discontent, worry, sadness, fear, shame, envy, loneliness, romantic love, love, peacefulness, contentment, optimism, joy, excitement, surprise.

Experiential marketing is aimed at generating positive emotions and feelings. These are among the key elements of this strategy. The FIVB beach volleyball experience provides joy, pleasure, excitement, and enthusiasm.

Sociocultural Benefits The sociocultural element is characterised by human thought emerging in the context of activities that are embedded in specific social and cultural settings (Dixon-Krauss, 1996). In this complex system, we will consider two relevant dimensions: first, values, and second, relationship and social interaction.

1. **Values.** In this context culture means the target audience's values stimulated by the brand. The promise should be consistent with

the values. In the context of brands, satisfaction relates to the meaning that a brand, service, or product embodies. In a previous section, we presented the Rokeach Value Survey, which measures two sets of values. The set of terminal values should be considered at this stage because they are culturally oriented. Terminal values associated with the FIVB beach volleyball experience are

- a sense of accomplishment,
- a world at peace,
- a world of beauty,
- an exciting life,
- freedom,
- happiness,
- pleasure, and
- self-respect.

2. **Relationship and social interaction.** The targeted audience derives a social brand satisfaction from group association and recognition, as it is part of human nature to form groups and subgroups. Its helps to define group membership and territory and common symbols. Type of brand satisfaction relies on the recognition and understanding of a group identity, to satisfy needs for socialisation. Potential social benefits generated by the FIVB beach volleyball experience are friendship, lifestyle, forming a group identity, and a sense of belonging.

Psychological Benefits (Self-Image) Psychological benefits are essentially personal as they fulfil the need for individualisation. This could refer to a sense of personal achievement or self-expression. Psychological benefits generated by FIVB beach volleyball are achievement, performance, mental stimulation, and self-expression.

The FIVB beach volleyball experiential promise is summarised in table 2.9.

The essence of the brand is that which summarises the benefits of the brand across all media types to all stakeholders. The experiential value of the brand is directly related to the emotional and sociocultural benefits.

Specifying the Overall Implementation Theme A brand theme is a conceptual driver that all the elements of a brand message can be connected with. It links the positioning and value promise to actual implementation. Organisations use themes to provide mental anchors and reference points. These reference points allow the consumer to place an organisation in a wider context and to distinguish its position. Themes can be expressed most pointedly if (a) they are used as prototypical expressions of an organisation's core values or mission, or of a brand character; (b) they are repeated and adapted over time; and (c) they are developed into a system of interrelated ideas.

Schmitt and Simonson (1997) stress a strategic issue in theme selection: the number of themes that an organisation wants to create for itself or its products. In the case of FIVB, the decision was to use multiple themes with the following architecture.

- "Keep the ball flying", "competition", "team spirit", "fair play", and "get involved" as overall themes for FIVB
- "Entertainment" and "sand, sun and sky" in association with "keep the ball flying" and "get involved" for beach volleyball

The overall theme is important because it provides the input for the implementation elements and states the sequence of the elements.

Table 2.9 **FIVB Beach Volleyball Experience Promise**

Tangible benefits	Major competitions, skills, fitness, physical beauty, entertainment, safety, comfort, responsive service
Emotional benefits	Joy, pleasure, excitement, and enthusiasm
Sociocultural benefits	• A sense of accomplishment, a world at peace, a world of beauty, an exciting life, freedom, happiness, pleasure, and self-respect • Friendship, lifestyle, forming group identity, and a sense of belonging
Psychological benefits	Achievement, performance, mental stimulation, and self-expression

Choosing and Designing Brand Experience Mediums in Relation to Experience Profile

In the previous chapter, we defined a brand as an entity that possesses a relation with a sport organisation's stakeholders. Within the framework of experiential marketing, this relation is qualified by the experience provided. It appeals to sensations, emotions, cognition, and action. Consequently, as a marketer you need to specify the benefits in relation to the kind of stimulation you are looking for. Your target audience can be stimulated through its senses; you can also aim at creating feelings and thoughts and encouraging people to act physically or communicate with others (table 2.10).

The experiential framework considers the global interaction between the targeted audience and the environment. This is a 360° stimulation designed to deliver the experiential promise (see figure 2.9).

According to Schmitt (1999), the instantiation of the strategic sense, feel, think, act, and relate modules occurs by means called "experience providers", for example communications, visual and verbal identity and signage, people, Web sites and electronic media, spatial environment, product presence, and cobranding. An experience is holistic; consequently these have to be integrated in a coherent and evolving system. Being highly relational, holistic theories do not see the sum of the parts as adding up to the whole. In this framework, individual elements of a system are determined by their relations to all other elements.

As a manager you must choose and design the experience mediums in order to deliver the benefits, for example physical, cognitive, emotional, sociocultural, and self-expressive. From a generic point of view an OSO brand can use a number of experience mediums, as explained next.

Services Services can be broadly defined as "deeds, processes and performance" (Zeithaml and Bitner, 2003). Services offered by an OSO are not tangible. Depending on the core business, a service can be a training session, a contest, an event, and so on. Services may include tangible elements such as facilities, Web sites, and instructional materials. A service can be viewed as a process that creates benefits for the users. A *process* is a naturally occurring or designed sequence of operations or events, possibly taking up time, space, expertise, or other resources that produce some outcome. So, a person attending a sport event needs to become informed, to book the ticket, to get to the stadium, and so forth. Consequently the organisation must manage a process aimed at fulfilling spectator expectation. In this context, perceived performance is dependent on the capacity to fulfil the spectator's service expectations.

Thus an OSO develops a range of deeds, products, resources, and facilities, and a process aimed at providing the desired experience to its stakeholders. The services offered are organised in a complex system including tangible and intangible elements. Those elements are experience providers.

Table 2.10 Experience Profile

Experience dimensions	Goals
Sense	To appeal to the senses with the objective of creating sensory experiences through sight, sound, touch, taste, and smell
Feel	To create an affective experience with the brand
Think	To create cognitive problem-solving experiences engaging customers creatively (convergent or divergent thinking)
Act	To enhance customers' physical experience, showing them alternative behaviour, lifestyle, or interactions
Relate	To relate the personal experience to other individuals in order to establish strong brand relation and brand communities

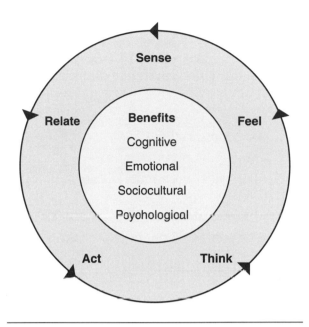

Figure 2.9 Strategic experience mediums related to benefits.

For event spectators, FIVB and local promoters provide a service based on high-level sport entertainment. They bring on the best players[6] in the world in the best locations, such as Copacabana (Brazil). The service is related to the following dimensions: events, facilities, design and aesthetics, people, communication, and cobranding. Furthermore, in order to bring the right experience to spectators or sponsors, cheerleaders, samba musicians, and dancing girls are an important part of the service.

Events An event is a powerful social factor that gathers different parties such as participants, audience, and sponsors in a sort of collective celebration to attend a sport or cultural type of entertainment. From an experiential perspective, events are key experience mediums because they generate emotions and social bonds. Furthermore, they build the base of sponsorship. We develop this marketing strategy in the last chapter.

There are different event types: sport spectacles (competitions involving top athletes) and participative (marathons as mass events) contests. These can have a worldwide impact (Olympic Games) or a local one. Street events are a new trend consisting of organising micro events in public places in order to entertain and involve the audience.

Events are part of the core service for FIVB. There are two beach volleyball official events: the World Tour and the World Championships. The World Tour is a global series of events that is staged in famous locations starring professional athletes from over 60 countries who compete for Olympic qualification, prize money, and world ranking. The World Tour runs over the full 12 months of the year and is positioned as "the joy of life". The World Championships are positioned as "the ultimate title". Staged every two years, it features the brightest stars of the World Tour. Furthermore, FIVB in conjunction with various partners has created special events such as a world congress, a world gala, fairs, and tailored events.

Facilities In some extended sport facilities there are tangible aspects: stadium, sport gymnasium, office, hospitality stands, and so on. As spatial and functional environments, these affect consumer experience and should be carefully designed.

The FIVB Beach Volleyball World Tour organisers must follow very detailed guidelines described in a handbook. The venue setup is described in minute detail in order to ensure such aspects as safety, accreditation, and access control; weather protection with roofed bleachers; properly equipped media centres; defined and controlled areas; seating; and hospitality requirements.

The setup and look of the game as well as the quality of the infrastructure and the organisation must ensure that all stakeholders are placed in the best possible environment and conditions to enjoy the event.

Design and Aesthetics Schmitt and Simonson (1997) describe how "corporate and brand aesthetics, i.e. attractive visual and other sensory markers and symbols that represent the organisation and its brands, appropriately dazzle customers through sensory experience". Their book, *Marketing Aesthetics,* offers a comprehensive strategic overview and implementation of corporate and brand identity management through aesthetics. As a marketer it is important to take an interest in the aesthetic value of an object.

---

[6] Players get prize money (e.g., $5,000,000) for the World Tour with equal opportunity for both genders.

FIVB Beach Volleyball World Tour marketing aesthetics refers to the marketing of sensory experiences and can be managed through different areas:

- Brand and sub-brand name: FIVB Beach Volleyball World Tour
- Specific logo (Internet address) and signage
- Environment: facilities (presented previously), materials (inflatable balloons), sound (music, speakers), shows (dancing girls, one-man show), colours (blue, yellow), hot temperature (and people spraying cold water on the spectators), and the smell of the sand
- Products: licensing and merchandising programmes, run by FIVB with its sponsors and partners, to reinforce the World Tour impact (see later section on licensing and merchandising)

People   The service is primarily delivered by OSO staff in relation to the stakeholders. This can be a source of a competitive advantage or a weakness. Another important aspect refers to the fact that other community members, participants, staff, athletes, and personalities, among others, can be powerful providers of experience. Experience occurs on a social base. It is about relationship and emotion.

Everyone involved in the FIVB Beach Volleyball World Tour, such as the players, spectators, staff, and dancers, is a young adult impassioned about sport. These people lead an active life, directed towards entertainment and fitness. They are heavy consumers and travel a great deal. They are interested in different forms of cultural expression, such as cinema and music. They live in big cities and match the "Defini" lifestyle established by Eurisko (www.eurisko.it). It is important to stress that these people are part of the service and provide certain sociocultural benefits. This is an important competitive advantage.

Communication   Experiential communication considers all sources of OSO contacts with its stakeholders. It refers to internal and external communication. The primary tools used are personal contact, advertising, publicity, flyers, events, public relations, direct marketing, and electronic media.

In the context of Beach Volleyball World Tour, FIVB and its partners—local promoter, broadcasters, and sponsors—launch above-the-line and below-the-line communications programmes. The following mediums are included:

1. Direct marketing
2. Sales promotion
3. Printed documents: flyers and catalogues
4. Advertising: posters, radio and TV
5. Publicity (e.g., media guides with the best players)
6. Public relations
7. Special events and shows (beach volleyball clinics with celebrities and coaches, Pro-Am, etc.)
8. Electronic media: Web site, SMS, MMS
9. Tailored TV and radio programmes
10. Contests
11. Music production

The FIVB is cautious of the importance of relationship marketing. This continuous process is aimed at developing cooperative programmes involving various stakeholders and fans. These provide an ideal platform for creating the right experience for fans, players, and sponsors.

Cobranding   Cobranding is a form of cooperation between two or more brands with a medium- to long-term duration, in which an additional value is created by the association. As an experience provider, cobranding has two levels.

- Value endorsement: The shared value creation and the strength of relationship is such as to create endorsement of one brand value by the other, with a strong affinity.
- Complementary competence: The two powerful and complementary brands come together and combine for a product or service that is more than the sum of its parts and that relies on each partner's committing a selection of its core skills and competencies to a product.

The FIVB offers marketing opportunities in relation to major events, annual competitions, special tailored events, and development programmes. As the sole owner of all commercial, television, and Internet rights for its properties, FIVB provides an exclusive cobranding platform. This includes sponsorship, alliances and partnership, licensing, and social cause cooperative arrangements. In the context of the Beach Volleyball World Tour, packages are tailored according to the needs of FIVB partners, including net tape exposure, on-court advertising panel exposure, Web site, poster and press release exposure, and product exclusivity. The FIVB partners belong to the beach volleyball fan consumption universe and launch activation programmes in order to provide a positive experience, for example through contests, Web site chat, exclusive programmes, and gadgets.

Licensing and Merchandising Licensing and merchandising in sport constitute a growing, highly sophisticated $17 billion business worldwide. Both refer to brand extension, which allows a marketer to use a successful brand name to launch a new or modified product in a same broad market. This strategy can be associated with cobranding (replica shirt with the official supplier).

With its partners, FIVB uses licensing and merchandising as powerful experience providers. In the Beach Volleyball World Tour, sponsors provide free T-shirts for spectators and launch specific merchandise items, for example those of Mikasa, the official game ball supplier (www.mikasasports.co.jp).

Quality Management System

An invisible element exists that makes it possible to conceive and deliver the promised experience. Indeed, an OSO must conceive and implement an organisation system aimed at managing quality. As noted in the previous chapter, Aaker (1996) defines perceived quality as the "idea that a consumer develops of the quality of a product or a service depending on his expectations and the comparisons that he can make with competing brands". In this context, highly perceived quality means that the OSO targeted audience's experiential expectations are fulfilled through long-term experience related to the brand.

The ISO 9000:2000[7] series is based on eight quality management principles that in turn form the basis of the quality management system standards. A quality management principle is a comprehensive and fundamental rule or belief for leading and operating an organisation, aimed at continually improving performance over the long term by focusing on the target audience while addressing the needs of all stakeholders. Among these principles, the process approach should be highlighted. According to this principle, a desired result is achieved more efficiently when activities and related resources are managed as a process. As a result, the value for the customer is due to a series of competencies and tasks. This is one of the major challenges for experience marketing implementation.

Conclusion

Olympic sport organisations should consider experiential marketing as an alternative to traditional marketing. For implementing this we have developed a four-step process aimed at specifying the elements presented in figure 2.10.

The OSO brand platform is the single source for all experiential marketing activities. These aim at creating and reinforcing a relationship with a targeted audience, which can be members, participants, sympathisers, individuals, sponsors, local authorities, or media. This relationship is based on an experience specified by four categories of benefits: cognitive, emotional, sociocultural, and psychological. Both emotional and sociocultural benefits are the core of the experience. For these to occur, the targeted audience needs to be stimulated through sense, feel, think, act, and relate strategies using experience providers.

We have illustrated each step of this framework with reference to FIVB beach volleyball. This is a good example of the benefits of experiential marketing. "Marketing is the process of planning and executing the conception, pricing, promotion, and distribution of ideas, goods, and services to create exchanges that satisfy individual and organisational objectives" (AMA). So, you must consider the fact that your audience is both rational and experiential. Consequently, traditional marketing aimed at delivering cognitive benefits is not over.

---

[7] www.iso.ch/iso/en/iso9000-14000/iso9000/qmp.html

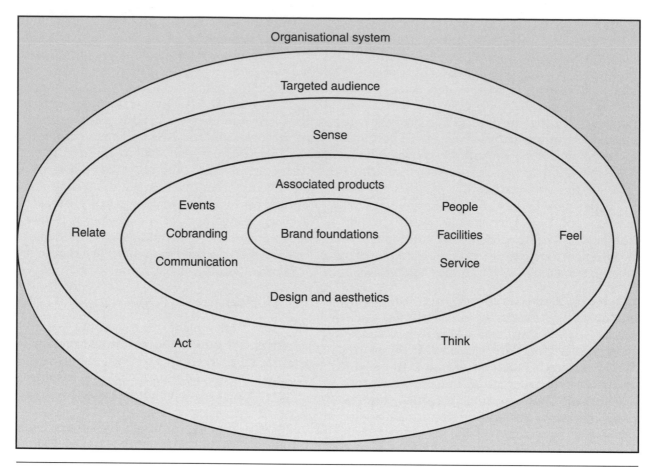

Figure 2.10 Experiential marketing layer design.

2.3 Conclusion

Olympic sport organisation marketers must understand how consumers reach decisions if they are to influence them and design a satisfactory service. On the one hand, experiential marketing expresses an evolution of method and techniques aimed at understanding consumers. On the other hand, it provides a framework for designing an attractive offer. In sport, the consumer is not always rational. The OSOs should analyse emotions, relationships, and the offer's sensorial perception in order to analyse sport consumers' behaviour and the decision-making process. Consequently, sport experience more and more integrates emotional, cultural, and social components. Nevertheless, the sponsors' decision-making process is becoming more and more rational. Consequently OSOs should work both on tangible benefits and on experiential ones.

In this chapter we used the word "consumer" to refer to individuals, sponsors, participants, and OSO members or sympathisers. "Consumer" has a business connotation, and the majority of OSOs are more focused on social goals. Andreasen[8] (1995) defines social marketing as "the application of commercial marketing technologies to the analysis, planning, execution, and evaluation of programmes designed to influence the voluntary behaviour of the target audiences in order to improve their personal welfare and that of their society". This quote stresses the fact that marketing concepts and methods can be used to fulfil both social and commercial goals. From a social perspective, marketing has the following characteristics.

[8] www.social-marketing.org/

- It aims at changing people's behaviour.
- The social marketing campaign is tailored to the unique perspective, needs, and experiences of the target audience, hopefully with input from representative members of this group.
- It strives to create conditions in the social structure that facilitate the behavioural changes promoted.
- It relies upon commercial marketing concepts.

Consequently and most fundamentally, OSO social marketing must

- begin with the target audience,
- understand targets through preliminary market research,
- design an offer in order to provide to the targeted audience a satisfactory experience, and
- understand strategy and address the competition by positioning the desired behaviour as preferable to competing behaviours.

three

Managing an Olympic Sport Organisation's Marketing Strategy

Looking at strategic management issues for Olympic sport organisations, Chappelet (2004) clarified this issue and revealed how the concepts and tools of strategic management can be applied to entities within the Olympic system. Considering various authors, he "proposed a simple, pragmatic model directly inspired by original ideas on designing strategy practised during the 1970s at the Harvard Business School". It is based on the four questions presented in table 3.1. It is a circular process, and these questions can be placed in a circle: Analysis → Vision → Action → Control → Analysis.

According to Bourgeois (1980), there are three different strategies corresponding to different scopes and organisation levels (see figure 3.1). A corporate strategy defines the scope of an OSO in terms of the market[1] in which it competes. Business strategy is concerned with how an OSO competes within a particular market. It aims at creating a sustainable competitive advantage over the competitors. Functional strategies are the elaboration and implementation of business strategies through individual functions such as human resources, communication, and marketing. Consequently, marketing strategy refers to a functional strategy, in relation to business and corporate strategy.

Marketing has a different input at each level of the organisation. The role of marketing within corporate-level strategy is to maintain a consumer and stakeholder focus. Marketing managers should communicate the benefits of this type of culture, and they have to communicate this throughout the OSO. The role of marketing within business-level strategy is to position offerings and to make adjustments taking into account the changes in consumer expectations and changes in the competitive environment. Lambkin (2000) stresses that "the most direct application of marketing strategy occurs at the functional level, where marketing personnel are involved in the related management of individual brands and the interrelationship between brands. This area includes basic decisions on issues such as market segmentation, targeting and positioning".

Aaker (2001) uses the concept of strategic marketing management to qualify "a system designed to help management both precipitate and make strategic decisions, as well as creating strategic vision". This is a proactive system. Its role is to analyse the market evolution in order to identify new opportunities and make medium-term decisions. This is a base for developing operational marketing. It concerns

---

[1] The OSO market is related to its mission.

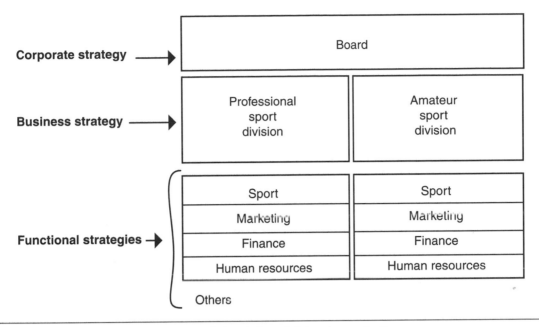

Figure 3.1 Olympic sport organisation strategic levels in a divisional organisation.

short-term strategies and actions related to the offer, promotion, distribution, and price. In brief, strategic marketing refers to analysis, and operational marketing refers to action.

The formulation of marketing strategy is generally thought of as a planning process. One of the well-accepted procedures was developed by Learned, Christensen, Andrews, and Guth (1965). In order to make your strategic decisions you should perform an internal and external analysis using the SWOT framework presented in the MEMOS strategic and performance management programme (Chappelet and Bayle, 2004). SWOT analysis is an effective way of identifying your strengths and weaknesses and of examining the opportunities and threats you face. Carrying out an analysis using the SWOT framework helps you to focus your activities into areas where you are strong and where the greatest opportunities lie. You will have to supplement this analysis with specific marketing dimensions.

We illustrate the different steps of this process with the case of a professional French soccer club: Olympique Lyonnais. It operates in the sport spectacle market, and we will focus on fans.

EXHIBIT 3.1 OLYMPIQUE LYONNAIS

- Soccer club founded in 1950
- Colours: blue and red
- President: Jean-Michel Aulas
- Winner of the French Championship three consecutive times (2002, 2003, 2004)
- UEFA Champions League quarter-finalist in 2003-2004
- Budget: 100 million euros
- 25 million euros invested in the player transfer in 2003-2004
- 3.5 million euros invested each year in the training centre
- Stadium: Gerland (41,852 seats)
- Average audience for the season 2003-2004: 35,717
- 23,000 season ticket holders
- Partnership between the OL association (34%) and SPCS (66%), created in 1998
- SPCS shareholders: Jean-Michel Aulas, 45%; Pathé Group, 34% (main club sponsor); Bruno Bonnell, 6% (Infogrammes chairman, another sponsor); and some members of the club management board, 6%

3.1 External Analysis

In the context of strategic marketing, external analysis involves an examination of the relevant elements external to an OSO. According to Aaker (2001), it is a question of taking into account the following dimensions:

- Consumer and stakeholder analysis: segmentation, expectations, unfulfilled needs, and so on
- Direct and indirect competitor analysis: strategies, performance, goals, strengths and weaknesses
- Market analysis: size, dynamics, barriers to entry, key success factors, and so on
- Environment analysis: political and legislative context, sociocultural trends, demographics, technology, and the like

You will identify opportunities and threats related to change. It is thus necessary to identify factors that are responsible for change and to make assumptions on the possible scenarios for the future.

Market Analysis

The sport organisation thus operates, first and foremost, in a market that is an area where buyers and sellers meet in order to carry out exchanges. According to Vernette (1998), a market can be defined according to four dimensions (see table 3.1):

1. Objects: What are we producing? What services do we offer?
2. Occupants: Who buys our products or services?
3. Occasions: When is the product or service consumed?
4. Objectives: Why is a product or service purchased?

The first dimension is the most classical. Olympic sport organisations essentially propose services that make it possible to practise and to attend sport. The second dimension refers to the characteristics of the persons who consume these services. Sport practice is wide, from various standpoints: age, sex, and sociological characteristics, among others. The third approach determines the time at which the product is consumed. Sport is a leisure activity because it is practised during free time, unlike the case for professional athletes. The fourth approach refers to consumer motives and expectations.

The first step of market analysis refers to the selection of the dimensions in order to analyse the market and constitutes a strategic choice for the sport organisation. This has two consequences: Targets could be different and competitors could be different. The second step is aimed at understanding the market's characteristics, dynamics, and attractiveness. These elements directly influence OSO activity. Some relevant questions:

- What is the size of the current and potential market?
- Is this market profitable?
- Is this market changing?
- Which are the distribution systems?
- Which are the key factors of success?

We will define the OL market based on the "object" and provide some key information about the French and European soccer

Table 3.1 Analysing the OL Market According to Its Four Dimensions

Market dimension	Characterisation of the market	Competitors
Object: What service do we propose?	French and European soccer spectacle market	Other French and European soccer clubs
Occupants: Who uses our services?	Mostly men (82%) from 10 to 65 years old	Any structure proposing services for men
Occasions: When are our services consumed?	Leisure market	Any structure proposing services related to free time
Objectives: Why do people buy our service?	Market related to expectations • Self-accomplishment • Enjoyment with friends	Any service likely to satisfy these expectations in the entertainment marketplace

spectacle market. We focus on stadium attendance and the TV audience, as well as key success factors (KSFs).

At the European level, soccer is the most popular sport, with 145 million followers. Soccer represents more than 60% of the 10 sporting events most followed in 2002 in the 60 countries on which the Eurodata TV Worldwide study is based. Soccer gets airtime on more than 600 TV channels. Attendance in the stadiums is progressing slightly (see table 3.2).

On a national basis, during the year 2003, 58.4% of the French over 14 years old followed soccer on TV with interest (see table 3.3). After a year of decrease, −7.9% in 2001-2002, attendance in stadiums increased +1.9%, with an average of 20,132 spectators per match.

These data demonstrate greater interest and an increase in the attendance in the stadiums. The KSFs for a soccer club are good sporting results, a large social base, a distinctive image, financial resources, efficient management, service, and continuous improvement. Loyal fans must not been taken for granted.

Consumer Analysis

Marketing is directed towards the consumer, which forces you to know and understand your actual and potential customers. It is a question of integrating the tools and methods presented in the preceding chapter in order to answer the following questions.

- Who are the most important customers? Who are the most profitable? Who are the most attractive potential customers?
- What are the motives of dissatisfaction and the unmet needs?
- What is the level of involvement?
- How can the market be segmented into groups?
- What kind of decision-making process do customers use?

Soccer consumers can be segmented into six groups according to their loyalty towards their favourite club and their involvement profile. Their characteristics are presented in table 3.4.

Table 3.2 **Top 10 European Premier League Attendance Evolution 2001-2002 and 2002-2003**

Rank	Country	Average	Evolution
1	England	35,464	+ 2.9%
2	Germany	33,794	+3.5%
3	Spain	28,593	+9.2%
4	Italy	25,474	−2.1%
5	France	19,757	−7.9%
6	Netherlands	16,255	+4.7%
7	Scotland	15,629	−2.3%
8	Russia	11,643	−6.1%
9	Sweden	10,161	+20.4%
10	Belgium	10,105	+10.1%

Table 3.3 **Five Top Sports Followed by the French**

2002			2003		
No.	Sport	%	No.	Sport	%
1	Soccer	49.5%	1	Soccer	58.4%
2	Tennis	38.4%	2	Tennis	37.2%
3	Cycling	28.6%	3	Rugby	27.3%
4	Rugby	28.0%	4	Track and field	23.5%
5	Track and field	24.9%	5	Cycling	23.1%

Source BVA

Table 3.4 **Soccer Consumer Segmentation**

	Season ticket holders	Distant fans	Regular	Disillusioned	Distant switchers	Opportunists
Loyalty	+++	+++	++	---	-	+
Interest, pleasure	+++	+++	++	+	+	+
Sign value	++	++	+	--	-	+
Perceived risk	+	+	++	+++	-	++
Profitability	+++	+	++	---	--	+
Development potential	+	+	+	+	-	+
Decision-making process	Habitual decision making or dissonance reducing	Habitual decision making or dissonance reducing	Dissonance reducing	Complex decision making	Limited decision making	Limited decision making

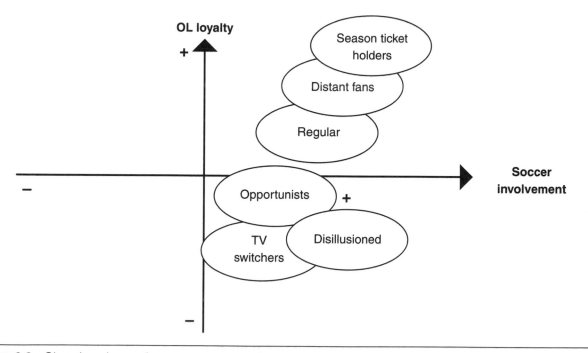

Figure 3.2 Olympique Lyonnais consumer segments.

Olympique Lyonnais consumers segmented according to their involvement and OL loyalty are presented in figure 3.2.

Individuals belonging to these segments have some common expectations in relation to the soccer spectacle. Without getting into a deep analysis, these fall into two dimensions: match and service offering. Table 3.5 summarises the main characteristics.

Competitor Analysis

In order to develop a marketing strategy you must identify and understand your competitors.

Table 3.5 **Soccer Fans' Common Expectations**

The match	Service offering
Two good teams involved in crucial game	Lively stadium
Goals	Stadium access and services
Players involved in showy soccer	Empathy (not being taken for granted)
Enthusiastic fans, flags, lively atmosphere	Responsiveness
A technical and respectful game	
A competent referee	

The first stage of the process is identification. The second stage aims at analysing competitors' strengths and weaknesses. We will present an operational framework in the next section focusing on competition field analysis.

This process should consider the strategic analysis based on Porter's five forces framework: the degree of rivalry among organisations, the buyer power, the supplier power, the threat to entry, and the threat of substitute. With a narrow focus, and as mentioned previously, competitor analysis is dependent upon the way the market is defined. Referring to OL, we are considering the soccer spectacle market. Direct competitors are clubs that are operating in the same catchment area and that have comparable activities, proposing comparable offers to the same target audience.

There are many direct competitors at the national and European levels. To identify those that are relevant, OL must consider the KSFs in this market, for example sporting results, distinctive image, and a large social base (e.g., attendance and positive attitude). In 2003, OL was ranked 29 (see table 3.6). It had increased its ranking from 47 to 29 (+18) in one year. The trend will be the same in 2004, due to OL's quarter-finalist position in the UEFA Champions League 2003-2004.

Olympique Lyonnais is far from the top European soccer club based on the number of fans. The leader is Real Madrid, followed by Juventus, Manchester United, Bayern Munich, and FC Barcelona. Based on stadium attendance, OL is ranked 34th in Europe and third in France behind Olympique de Marseille and Paris Saint-Germain FC (see table 3.7).

Consequently, OL's direct French competitors are Olympique de Marseille and Paris Saint-Germain FC. From a European perspective and based on its sport results, OL could challenge the top clubs.

Considering its popularity and its social base, and according to a Sportlab study performed in February 2004, OL competes with Olympique de Marseille and Paris Saint-Germain FC. Of the 3.5 million French declaring that they follow soccer with strong interest, 65% have a positive attitude towards OL. Considering the total population, OL (52% positive attitude) is ranked second behind Olympique de Marseille (53%). On a local basis, 47% of the population have a positive attitude (28% in 2002) and 10% don't like OL (20% in 2002). This result is mostly due to the 15–24- and +50-year-old groups and the women.

Some of the key questions to answer about competitors are these:

- What are their objectives and strategies?
- What is their image?
- What is their positioning?
- What action leverage can they use to increase their market capacity?
- What are their competitive advantages?
- What is the brand equity profile?

As mentioned previously, we will stress some of these elements in the section on competition field analysis.

Environmental Analysis

From a macro perspective, the environment in which the market is located should be analysed. This is a question of studying the following components: economic, legislative, cultural,

Table 3.6 **European Club Rankings 2003 (Based on European Cup, National League and Cup)**

New	Old	Clubs	Country	Points
1	1	Juventus FC	Italy	1,258.69
2	6	FC Bayern München	Germany	1,181.84
3	7	Real Madrid CF	Spain	1,164.62
4	8	Manchester United	England	1,154.04
5	3	FC Barcelona	Spain	1,151.90
6	4	FC Porto	Portugal	1,088.62
7	2	AC Milan 1899	Italy	1,032.22
8	19	SS Lazio	Italy	1,009.15
9	5	Ajax	Netherlands	1,003,25
10	30	Arsenal	England	967.11
11	9	Internazionale FC 1908	Italy	939.04
12	13	Parma AC	Italy	928.87
13	54	RC Deportivo de La Coruña	Spain	908.66
14	16	PSV	Netherlands	898.40
—	—	—	—	—
24	17	Paris Saint-Germain FC	France	797.57
29	47	Olympique Lyonnais de Lyon	France	726.14

and technological. These trends can present both threats and opportunities for OSOs.

Economics

Economic issues can affect marketing strategy, particularly economic growth and unemployment. Furthermore, some relevant information can be derived from leisure consumption.

At 0.2%, French GDP growth in 2003 was the lowest since 1993. The outcome for 2003 as a whole bore the scars of the difficult start to the year: Private dependent employment fell by 50,000, bringing about a rise of 0.4 points in the unemployment rate; meanwhile, the slowdown in public revenues brought the public deficit to 4.1% of GDP. In Europe, confidence was low while unemployment was high. As of this writing, Germany, Italy, and the Netherlands were in recession.

In 2000, four of five people said that they had practised at least one cultural activity. French people spent 3 hours and 40 minutes every day on their leisure activity. This is a growing trend. Young people, city dwellers, executives, and higher-education graduates are the largest consumers of cultural leisure. Last but not least, as the generations move on, more and more young people are accessing culture, especially girls.

Culture

Sociocultural research shows how societies evolve and identifies the main forces driving change in business. Such insights have a direct impact on marketing, human resources, and other corporate policies. Consequently OSOs should consider information such as the trends listed next. One can get this type of data from

Table 3.7 **European Clubs' Average Attendance 2003-2004**

No.	Club	Country	Attendance	No.	Club	Country	Attendance
1	BV 09 Borussia Dortmund	Ger	78,808	18	Valencia CF	Spa	46,000
2	Real Madrid CF	Spa	70,990	19	Club Atlético de Madrid	Spa	43,333
3	FC Barcelona	Spa	69,727	20	Liverpool	Eng	42,933
4	Manchester United	Eng	67,646	21	VfB Stuttgart 1893	Ger	42,256
5	AC Milan 1899	Ita	61,334	22	Fenerbahçe SK Istanbul	Tur	41,636
6	FC Schalke 04	Ger	61,103	23	Feyenoord	Neth	41,596
7	Celtic	Sco	58,437	24	Chelsea	Eng	41,254
8	Internazionale FC 1908	Ita	56,897	25	Everton	Eng	38,797
9	AS Roma	Ita	55,413	26	1. FC Köln	Ger	38,569
10	FC Bayern München	Ger	52,385	27	Arsenal	Eng	38,054
11	Newcastle United	Eng	51,927	28	Paris Saint-Germain FC	Fra	37,981
12	Olympique de Marseille	Fra	51,914	29	Hertha BSC Berlin	Ger	37,754
13	Glasgow Rangers	Sco	49,158	30	1. FC Kaiserslautern	Ger	36,817
14	Ajax	Neth	48,998	31	Leeds United	Eng	36,302
15	SS Lazio	Ita	48,989	32	SV Werder Bremen	Ger	35,956
16	Hamburger SV	Ger	46,961	33	Sevilla FC	Spa	35,357
17	Manchester City	Eng	46,730	34	Olympique Lyonnais	Fra	35,120

Sociovision,[2] CCA,[3] and elsewhere in order to discern actual or emerging current sociocultural trends affecting OSO activity.

As we stressed in chapter 2, Faith Popcorn has uncovered and studied cultural trends that will shape the future. Olympique Lyonnais should consider the following trends:

• Clanning: "Hitches us up with those who share our interests, ideas, aspirations and addictions" (Popcorn and Marigold,1996). Individuals are willing to be part of a group. They are inclined to join up, belong to, and hang out with groups of like kind, deriving a secure feeling that their own belief systems will somehow be validated by consensus. Soccer drives you to belong to a club, a "clan", or a "tribe", and you are proud of it.

• Fantasy adventure: Individuals crave low-risk excitement and stimulation to escape from stress and boredom. Soccer should bring positive emotions and feelings in a safe environment.

• Cocooning: Individuals are retreating into safe, cosy, homelike environments to shield themselves from the harsh realties of the outside world. Technology (TV, pay per view, Internet, SMS, MMS) allows soccer fans to be part of a virtual community and to get in touch with their clan.

• Vigilante consumers: These consumers are suspicious of corporate motives. They are tired of being wooed by advertisements full of false promises and tired of being taken for granted. They are declining to purchase when they don't like the company's policies.

Legal Issues

Legislative framework refers to the laws, decrees, and regulations in force in countries, which OSOs must consider. This is a complex issue, like politics. Questions to ask are the following:

• What are the legislative changes on the relevant level?

• What affects our activity?

Technology

Some technological trends or technological events have the potential to affect strategies. Leisure is highly affected by certain technological innovations: digital TV, satellites, Internet, mobile phones (SMS, MMS). Sustaining technology leads to improved performance of existing products and services; disruptive technology changes the business model and the nature of assets and competences needed to win.

The Internet is a good example of sustaining technology for soccer clubs. This medium allows people from all over the world to get connected (see figure 3.3). In France the sport Web site audience multiplied by three from 2000 to 2003. More than 8 million users connect to these Web sites. Among these are 2 million soccer fans.

The Internet can be a disruptive technology also. In 1999, a Forester report from Hardie and Charron titled "The Sports Power Shift" stressed the fact that the Web will shift control of the sport experience from broadcast networks to professional leagues. As bandwidth improves, leagues will rely on in-house programming and e-commerce to build profitable direct relationships with consumers and advertisers. These experts recommended the following:

• Rights holders need to unbundle digital from analogue rights.

• Broadcasters should invest in Web technology.

• Retailers should build online stores with leagues.

• Internet ad networks should tackle television.

• Athletes and agents should wake up to commerce (athlete Web sites).

Five years later, all these recommendations had been put into action.

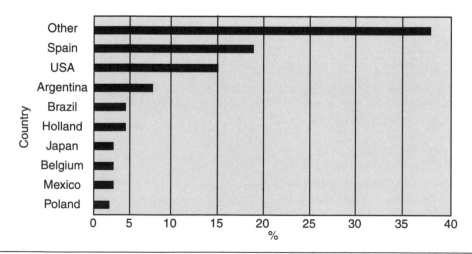

Figure 3.3 FCBarcelona.com visits in 2003.
Source FC Barcelona.

3.2 Internal Analysis: Resources and Competencies

As with external analysis, internal analysis should be performed in order to establish both corporate and business strategies. In view of the linking between the three strategic levels, we will consider the dimensions involved in assessing OSO resources and competencies. Strategic marketing issues bring a special focus on brand equity.

Mission, Values, Internal Culture, and System of Permanent Objectives

Chappelet (2004) develops these important issues in strategic management. The mission of OL is to belong to the top European club group from a sport and managerial point of view. The mission highlights that the sport company must be developed. The club chairman, Jean-Michel Aulas, is promoting a business-oriented culture: "managing the club like a firm". Values are ambition, sense of accomplishment, competence, responsibility, courage, excitement, and sense of belonging. A system of permanent objectives is established:

- To remain in the top three French clubs so as to qualify each year for the UEFA Champions League
- To be the richest French club
- To be sold out for every game

At an operational level, short-term objectives are the following:

- To win the French championship
- To qualify for the Champions League quarter-finals

Medium- and long-term objectives are these:

- To perpetuate the club at the top European level
- To improve club image and its attractiveness in order to
  - build a large social base;
  - increase the media exposure;
  - attract major sponsors, shareholders, and stakeholders; and
  - increase the financial resources of the club.

Organisational and Human Resources

On one hand, organisational and human resources refers to OSO strategy formalisation, activity planning, and system of control, as well as the informal relations between staff and departments. On the other hand, these resources are related to the internal structure, for example departments.

Olympique Lyonnais has 140 employees; 55% operate in the sporting sector and 45% in the management sector. This sector is under the president's and the board's responsibility. There are five functions: administration, communication, commercial, media, and marketing (see figure 3.4).

Olympique Lyonnais organisational resources are competent, involved, and well managed, with precise planning and efficient control. Their weakness is related to the split between communication, commercial, media, and marketing. Communication and media should be included in the marketing department.

Facilities

Physical resources initially relate to the geographical establishment of the organisation, its facilities, and its equipment. They can be an asset or a weakness for marketing action aiming at consumer satisfaction. Olympique Lyonnais is the owner of a training centre, the headquarters building, two shops for merchandise products, two restaurants, one travel agency, and one hairdresser.

The team uses Gerland Stadium, owned by the town of Lyons. Conceived by the architect Tony Garnier and built in 1913, this stadium was fully restructured in 1998 for the FIFA World Cup (project cost was 33 million euros). Gerland Stadium is a contemporary urban stadium where spectators are close to the pitch. This architecture provides a safe and emotional experience to the 41,051 fans.

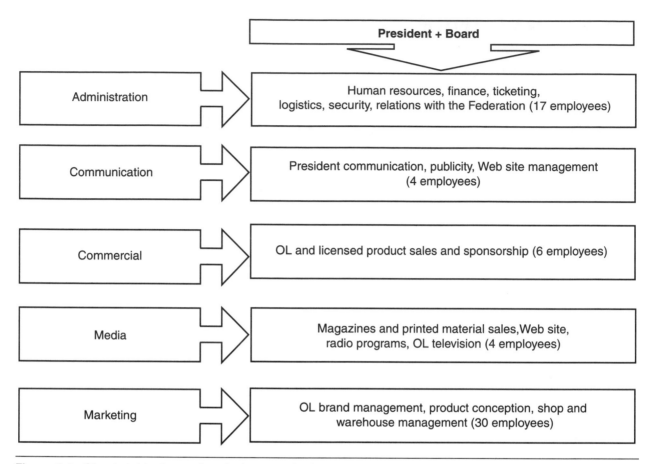

Figure 3.4 OL administration and marketing organisation.

Finance

Each sport organisation has a share of stockholders' equity and a possibility of loan banking. This volume determines its financial standing. This is a significant variable because marketing action can require the implementation of liquidities.

The OL budget for the 2003-2004 season was close to 100 million euros with a positive result. This is a good financial performance. The financial strengths of OL are a budget that is the highest in the French Premier League, positive results, and shareholders with a strong capacity to invest such as Pathé Group and Infogrammes. Nevertheless, this budget doesn't allow OL to compete with its main European competitors, Manchester United (251 million euros), Juventus (215 million euros), and Real Madrid (190 million euros). Furthermore this balance could be at risk due to the importance of UEFA Champions League income.

Sporting Results

Sporting results are the main KSF in soccer. As mentioned previously, OL is now the best French soccer club, as the winner three consecutive times in the French Championship (2001-2002; 2002-2003; 2003-2004) and UEFA Champions League quarter-finalist (2003-2004). Its challenge is to secure its position at a national and European level and to win the UEFA Champions League.

Brand Equity

We devoted the first chapter to OSO brand equity. From a marketing perspective this can be a strength or a weakness. Assessing each dimension yields important information in order to make strategic decisions. The brand equity of OL is summarised in table 3.8.

Table 3.8 **OL Brand Equity**

Dimensions	Olympique Lyonnais	Comments
Awareness	French fans' soccer club unprompted awareness 2003: • Paris Saint-Germain 80% • Olympique de Marseille 75% • Olympique Lyonnais 30%	• OL's score is far below those of Paris Saint-Germain and Olympique de Marseille • Awareness in progress in France due to OL sporting results • Suffers from a lack of awareness at a European level
Image	OL image has three dimensions: • A competitive club: good team, ambitious, good sporting result, champion, etc. • Well managed: competent, no scandals, good management • Distant and lofty (for non-OL fans)	• Positive image in France: competitive and well managed • Negative perception (e.g., distance for non-OL fans) is due to communication
Perceived quality	Fan expectation importance and OL performance assessed in relation to three dimensions: sport and team, stadium, services and products, and management (see results in figure 3.5)	• Good results for sport and team • Stadium access and cleanliness should be improved • Product range offer, responsiveness, empathy, and pricing policy should be improved • Management should improve its communication
Positive attitude	• 52% of French football fans have a positive attitude about OL (ranked second behind Olympique de Marseille: 53%) • 47% of the local population has a positive attitude (28% in 2002) and 10% don't like it (20% in 2002)	Positive linking in France, not the case at a European level
Relationship and loyalty	• Season ticket owner loyalty rate close to 90% • Nonseason ticket holders are increasing their participation in the stadium • 65% of the 3.5 million French soccer fans are following OL with interest	Results already high and improving year after year
Stakeholders	Strong partnership with the City of Lyons, Conseil Général du Rhône, sponsors, shareholders, and the French soccer governing body	This is one of OL's main assets
Legal protection	OL brand is a registered trademark	OL's position is secure due to efficient legal protection in France
"Corporate design"	Fans fancy OL logo, stadium architecture	OL's corporate design is a major concern for management; needs to be improved in order to be consistent with OL future positioning

OL brand equity assessment highlights some strengths and weaknesses. Its main assets at the French level are related to its image, sporting results, relationship with fans, and loyalty. Its major weaknesses are at a European level—lack of recognition and of social base.

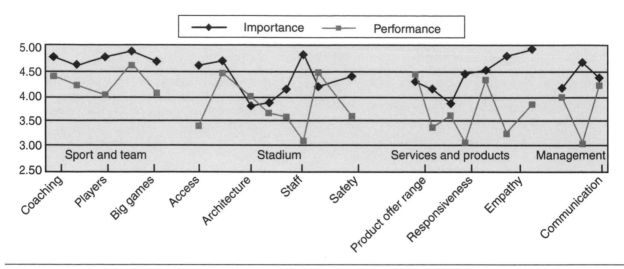

Figure 3.5 Olympique Lyonnais fans' perceived quality assessment.

EXHIBIT 3.2 OLYMPIQUE LYONNAIS SERVICE OFFERINGS

- Tickets and season tickets
- Licensed merchandise distribution
  - Planet OL
    - Two points of sale: one located in the city centre, two at the club headquarters next to the stadium
    - Another 800-m² Planet OL due by 2004
  - Web site
- Travel agency: OL Travel
  - Located in Planet OL (city centre)
  Provides services for fans for away matches
  Full range of products for holidays
- Two restaurants: the Seven'th and the Tony Garnier
- One men's hairdresser
- One television channel, OL TV, in collaboration with TLM, the local TV channel
  - Three programmes
    - A daily three-minute interview with a player at 8:00 pm
    - A 13-minute journal every evening without a match at 8:45 pm (except Monday)
    - Live programme before and after each match
  - Television viewership of 550,000 per week
- *Olympic One,* the official magazine (150,000 copies)

- "Platform OL", four pages distributed during each home match (25,000 copies)
- "Club Spirit", four pages for 1,500 VIPs
- OL Media, a department created to sell advertising spaces on these various supports
- Radio: Club OL
- OL Tour: event promotion in commercial malls with OL's main sponsors

3.3 Analysis of the Competition Field

The OSO market refers to sport practice and sport entertainment. It is a competitive market that should be analysed through the following dimensions: current competitors' marketing strategy strengths and weaknesses, OSO positioning, strategic segmentation, OSO generic strategies, tactics, offer versus market analysis, and OSO competitive advantage. The following sections develop each of these dimensions.

Competitor Strengths and Weaknesses Analysis

Identification of the competitive strengths carried out previously must be done at the level of the specific marketing dimensions. Competitor analysis is often complex. The first stage relates to the analysis of direct competitors. If necessary, one can analyse OSO indirect competitors and consider the threat of substitutes. Table 3.9 relates to the two main French competitors of OL as well as three at the European level.

Table 3.9 **OL Direct Competitors' Strengths and Weaknesses**

	Strengths	Weaknesses
Olympique de Marseille	• Image • Awareness • Local social base • Attendance • Positive attitude	• Sporting results • Managerial performance • International social base
Paris Saint-Germain	• National social base • Located in Paris	• Sporting results
Real Madrid	• Image • Awareness • Top players: celebrities • Enduring sporting performance • International social base • Tradition	• Managerial performance • Sporting results (season 2003-2004)
Manchester United	• Image • Awareness • Top players • Managerial performance • International social base • Attendance • Service perceived quality	• Sporting results could be better
AC Milan	• Image • Awareness • Top players • Tradition • Attendance	• Sporting results could be better • Managerial performance

Current Positioning

The concept of positioning emerged at the beginning of the 1970s, when Al Ries and Jack Trout wrote a series of articles titled "The Positioning Era" for *Advertising Age*. They specify that positioning does not correspond to making a good product. Positioning is what you make in the target audience's mind. Olympic sport organisation positioning is in relation to its competitors. It refers to the customers' perceptions of the place a product or brand occupies in a market segment. We stress that brand identity refers to the way an OSO wants to be perceived. At this stage, the question of what is important determines the current positioning.

Positioning refers to the place an offering occupies in the consumer's mind on important attributes relative to competitive offerings. There are two approaches:

• Head-to-head positioning involves competing directly with competitors on simi-

lar attributes in the same target market (soccer clubs).

• Differentiation positioning involves seeking a less competitive, smaller market niche in which to locate a brand (FIVB beach volleyball).

EXHIBIT 3.2 BUILDING A PERCEPTUAL MAP

Generally, the organisation brand positioning process involves these steps:

1. Identifying competing OSO brands.
2. Identifying the attributes that define the brand "space" through in-depth interviews.
3. Collecting information from a sample of fans about their perceptions of each brand on the relevant attributes through questionnaires or interviews (they are asked to rate the match between each attribute and their perception of the brand using a scale from 1 [totally disagree] to 5 [fully agree]).

4. Determining each OSO's brand space using a graph.

5. Determining each brand's current location in relation to the others. This can be done using a simple radar graph (see figure 3.6) or perceptual mapping techniques. These graphic techniques attempt to visually display the perception of customers or potential customers. Typically the position of a brand is displayed relative to the competition. Perceptual maps can have any number of dimensions but most commonly have two dimensions. Any more dimensions are a challenge to draw and confusing to interpret. An assortment of statistical procedures can be used to convert the raw data collected in a survey into a perceptual map, for example factor analysis and multi-dimensional scaling.

Positioning is described by parameters that are important to the consumers. Therefore, it is advisable to use in-depth interviews to deter-mine relevant parameters in order to understand how customers are assessing different soccer club brands. The number of relevant attributes is normally low. Fans are looking for a club that they perceive as international; one that has top sporting results (winner); and one that is prestigious, passionate, well managed, and user friendly and has panache and a tradition. The head-to-head positioning of OL in relation to its two main French competitors and three top European clubs is presented in figure 3.6.

Results show that Manchester United has the strongest positioning. Olympique Lyonnais has a unique strong attribute—well managed. None of the competitors have the perfect profile. There seems to be a contradiction between prestige, top sporting results, and cautious financial management. These data refer to global positioning. The situation can vary with different fan segments. According to the main segment attributes, a club can decide to match with a

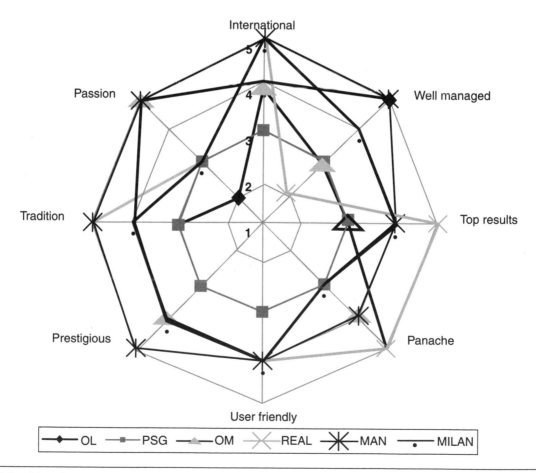

Figure 3.6 Olympique Lyonnais positioning.

particular segment. This strategy is not relevant for a soccer club because the soccer club needs a large social impact at a national and an international level.

Strategic Segmentation

Strategic segmentation "is based on an analysis of the competencies required in order to be competitive in a given segment. It seeks to carry out a split that will make it possible to allocate resources in the most sensible way" (Détrie et al., 1997). An OSO must analyse its situation according to its market in order to choose its targets and deploy the financial, human, technical, and material resources to create a service offering whose value is superior to that of the competition. This is a six-step process.

1. Segmentation criterion choice
2. Strategic options assessment
3. Offering target selection
4. Development of the marketing mix for the segment
5. Implementation of the marketing plan
6. Monitoring and control

We shall focus on the phase relating to the choice of one or several targets for the services that the sport organisation offers. In order to do so, we adapt the General Electric/McKinsey nine-cell portfolio. The two axes of the matrix presented in figure 3.7 are segment attractiveness and OSO competitiveness.

Three regions show strategic recommendations:

- Targeted segments are those that an OSO ranks high on both dimensions and have an excellent profit (social, financial, or both) potential.
- "Don't go" segments are those that rank low in both dimensions and have poor prospects (no investment).
- Selective segments correspond to three cells: average attractiveness and average competitiveness, high attractiveness and low competitiveness, low attractiveness and high competitiveness. They are not a priority for OSOs.

For OL, the attractiveness of the segments (identified during the segmentation phase) is determined by criteria such as the following:

- Fit with the club mission
- Segment size (number of persons)
- Level of involvement towards soccer
- Buying power and expenditure related to soccer
- Trend for the future (growth or decline)
- Service perceived quality
- Capability to improve service perceived quality
- Club positioning in the marketplace

Olympique Lyonnais competitiveness is computed on the basis of several criteria. The club performance relates to

- the existence of direct and indirect competitors,

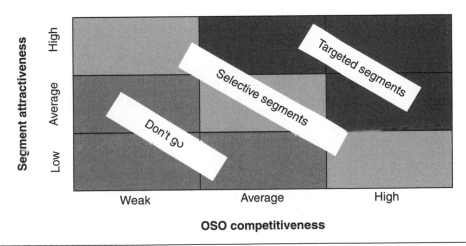

Figure 3.7 Segment attractiveness versus competitiveness matrix.

- the competitors' capability to satisfy expectations, and
- the financial risk.

Results of the analysis carried out for OL are presented in table 3.10.

Placing each segment on the matrix as shown in figure 3.8 provides a clearer picture.

Table 3.10 **Criteria Related to Segment Attractiveness and Performance for OL**

Criteria	STH	DIF	REG	DIS	MSW	OPP	DCF
Attractiveness							
Segment size	+	+++	++	+	+++	++	+++
Loyalty towards the club	+++	++	++	---	-	-	---
Level of involvement towards soccer	+++	+++	++	++	+	+	+++
Buying power	+/+++	+/++	+/+++	---	---/+	--/+	+/+++
Future trend	+	++	++	?	++	++	++
Service perceived quality	++	++	++	---	+	+	-
Capability to improve perceived quality	++	+	++	++	+	+	+
Club positioning in the marketplace	+++	+++	++	---	+	++	-
Fit with OSO mission	+++	+++	+++	+++	+++	+++	++
Performance							
Number of direct and indirect competitors	+++	+++	+++	+++	+++	+++	+++
Competitors' perceived quality	+	+/++	+/++	+/+++	+/+++	+/+++	-/+++
Financial risk	+	+	+	+	+	+	++

STH: Season ticket holders; DIF: distant fans; REG: regular fans; DIS: disillusioned; MSW: media switchers; OPP: opportunists; DCF: direct competitors' fans.

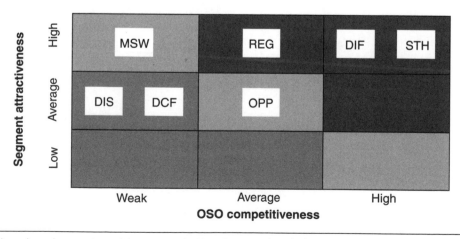

Figure 3.8 Olympique Lyonnais matrix segment attractiveness in relation to competitiveness.

Diagnostic About the Current Generic Strategies

Porter (1980) has argued that an organisation's strengths fall under two headings: cost advantage and differentiation. By applying these strengths in either a broad or narrow scope, generic strategies result in cost leadership, differentiation, and focus. Depending on an OSO's functional organisation, these strategies are applied at the business unit or at a departmental level (marketing).

Cost leadership strategy calls for being the low-cost producer in a marketplace for a given level of quality. This strategy is used by some operators in some competitive sport and leisure businesses such as fitness. Some of the ways that organisations acquire cost advantage is by improving process efficiency. This strategy is not relevant for the soccer business market because the KSFs are sport results, top players, functional stadium, and modern facilities, among others, and fans are willing to pay more for this.

A differentiation strategy calls for the development of an OSO brand and service offering unique attributes that are valued by consumers and that customers perceive to be better than, or different from, the competition. The value added by the uniqueness of the product may allow the organisation to charge a premium price for it. Most top soccer clubs are running this kind of strategy. They are investing a lot in top players, hoping that the higher price will cover the extra costs incurred in offering the unique experience.

Focus strategies concentrate on a narrow segment, and within that segment they attempt to achieve either a cost advantage or differentiation. The premise is that focusing entirely on a particular segment can better satisfy its expectations. This kind of strategy is not relevant for professional soccer clubs in general or OL in particular because these clubs need to build a large social base at a local, national, and international level.

The KSFs for a top soccer club drive these organisations to develop a differentiation strategy. They are putting their finances at risk, and most are in deep debt. Olympique Lyonnais is not in this category; due to its cautious management it is making profits.

Current Tactics Related to Competitor Analysis

This aspect leads marketing strategists to consider the OSO position in the marketplace in order to react to its competitors. There are four typical strategies in relation to competitors: leader, challenger, follower and specialist.

Tactics of a Leader

The leader has a significant competitive advantage, for example a dominant position in the marketplace, better resources, and capabilities forming its distinctive competencies. These competencies enable innovation, efficiency, quality, and fan loyalty, all of which can be leveraged to create a cost advantage or a differentiation advantage. According to Marion et al. (2003), a leader can aim to

- improve the global position of its sector, trying to increase the demand—for example, number of fans and fan expenses;
- make the fans loyal and involve competitors' fans; and
- dissuade new organisations from getting into the marketplace.

Olympique Lyonnais is acting as a leader in the French marketplace based on its sport results and its financial power (highest of First League: 100 million euros).

Tactics of a Challenger

The challenger is ranked second in the marketplace, and its ambition is to become the leader. Marion et al. (2003) recommend two types of attack.

- The frontal attack consists of attacking the leader on its most significant segment of customers. To do this it is necessary to invest significant human and financial resources.
- The side attack concentrates on the weak points of the offer of the leader. If it is successful, it will be able afterward to attack the leader on its major fan segments.

In soccer, it is difficult to attack the leader club local social base. On the other hand, it is possible to attack its distant fans by getting top sport results and good positioning. From this perspective, OL is acting as a challenger in the European marketplace.

Tactics of a Follower

The follower strategy is characterised by adaptation of the successful processes used by a successful organisation, in and out of the marketplace, and is a weak innovation. In addition, it is not very ambitious with regard to market share, instead developing activities in the leader share. In order to reach its goals the organisation is likely to use the two following tactics:

- A lower price for a similar offer (this is not relevant for a soccer club)
- Improving offer quality by analysing the mistakes made by the leader trying to innovate

This second tactic is relevant for most soccer club services, and OL is "playing it safe", taking lessons from its top competitors' mistakes.

Tactics of a Specialist

The specialist is located in a "niche" where fans are willing to pay heavily for a service aimed at satisfying their specific expectations. According to Kotler, Dubois, and Manceau (2003), in order to be profitable and durable a niche must

- have a critical size with reference to buying power,
- have a significant growth potential,
- be one that is ignored or has been abandoned by the competition,
- correspond to organisation distinctive competences, and
- be able to defend its position in case of attack from competitors.

This kind of strategy is not relevant for any professional soccer club. At this stage, we can make an intermediate synthesis with respect to the current strategies used by OL and two of its competitors at both the national and the international level (table 3.11).

Offer Versus Market Analysis

To portray alternative growth strategies we can use the Ansoff matrix (figure 3.9) (1965). This well-known marketing tool was first published in the *Harvard Business Review* in an article titled "Strategies for Diversification". Marketers who have objectives for growth use this strategy.

Market Penetration

With market penetration we market our existing products and services to our existing customers. Management seeks to increase its market share with the current product range. Products and services are not altered. This is the least risky of all methods of expansion, and opportunities include the following:

- Encouraging existing customers to buy more of the OSO brand
- Encouraging customers who are buying a competitive brand to switch to the OSO brand
- Encouraging nonusers within the segment to buy the OSO brand

Market Development

With market development we market our existing product range in a new market. This means that the product remains the same but is marketed to a new audience (marketing to a new geographic territory). New segments can be addressed directly or by marketing through

Table 3.11 Current Olympic Lyonnais, Paris Saint-Germain, and Real Madrid FC Tactics

Clubs	Generic strategies	Tactics
Olympique Lyonnais	Differentiation	Leader strategy in France; challenger and follower strategy in Europe
Real Madrid	Differentiation	Leader strategy at a national and international level
Paris Saint-Germain	Differentiation	Challenger strategy at a French level and at a European level

new or additional channels of distribution (Internet).

Offer Development

Offer development refers to a new product to be marketed to our existing customers. Existing products can be improved, or if the OSO has sufficient resources, altogether new products can be developed to match existing market expectations.

Diversification

With diversification we market completely new products to new customers. There are two types of diversification, namely related and unrelated diversification. With related diversification, the OSO remains in a market with which it is familiar (sport merchandise for a sport club). Unrelated diversification refers to a situation in which we have no previous industrial or or market experience (travel packages). This carries the highest risk of all strategies.

Table 3.12 presents an Olympique Lyonnais Ansoff matrix established for the years 2000 to 2004.

The hypotheses for the next quadrennial are presented in the following matrix (table 3.13).

Figure 3.9 The Ansoff matrix.

Table 3.12 **2001-2004 OL Ansoff Matrix**

	Existing offer	New offer
Existing markets	• Sport entertainment (season and single) ticket • Merchandise product • Web site • Events	• Travel agency • Restaurants
New markets	• Web site • Merchandise product sales • Magazines	• Hairdressers • Travel agency

Table 3.13 **2005-2008 OL Ansoff Matrix**

	Existing offers	New offers
Existing markets	See exhibit 3.2	• Loyalty card • Information through mobile phones (SMS and MMS) • Customised product merchandise
New markets	• Targeting French and European fans through media: TV, Web, radio, magazines • Fan cards	• Licences for merchandised products: "city wear"

Competitive Advantage Analysis

Differentiation aims at creating or maintaining one or several competitive advantages. A competitive advantage corresponds to the characteristic or attribute set held by the product or the brand that confers on it a degree of superiority in connection with the most direct competitors (Lambin, 2002). According to Porter (1980), a competitive advantage exists when an OSO is able to deliver the same benefits as competitors but at a lower cost (cost advantage), or deliver benefits that exceed those of competing offers (differentiation advantage). (We are using the expression "sustainable and defensible competitive advantage" [SDCA] to underline the fact that the OSO is acting in a changing competitive environment and that the question is one of being organised to sustain and to reinforce its position.) Creation and development of SDCA depend on the following dimensions:

- Your competition strategy (offer, positioning, communication, sales, etc.)
- Your assets and weaknesses with reference to your competitors
- The marketplace
- Your competitors

The question is one of integrating in your analysis four fields relating to the way you are competing, the basis of the competition, the market characteristics, and your competitors. In this context, your competitive advantages relate to your resources and competences in connection with the forces and the weaknesses of your direct and indirect competitors. Principal dimensions likely to create an SDCA are presented in table 3.14.

Table 3.14 **Factors Creating or Likely to Create a Competitive Advantage**

Factors	Characteristics
Offer perceived quality	SERVQUAL dimensions • Tangible elements: appearance of physical facilities, equipment, personnel, and communication materials • Reliability: ability to perform the promised service dependably and accurately • Responsiveness: willingness to help customers and provide prompt service • Assurance: knowledge and courtesy of employees and their ability to convey trust and confidence; reliability • Empathy: caring, individualised attention provided to customers and stakeholders Additional characteristics • OSO performance (financial, social, managerial, sporting results, etc.) • Stakeholders
Price	• Level related to competitors • Flexibility: according to the period, to loyalty, etc.
Communication	• Strategy and communication mix (including events, etc.)
Sales and distribution network	• Accessibility • Availability • Reactivity • Personalisation • Expertise
Intangible elements	• Image • Positioning
Geographic territory	• Size • Localisation • Proximity
Knowledge and relationship	• Awareness • Positive attitude • Bonding

During the last three years, OL has developed competitive advantages:

- Sport performance: French Championship in three consecutive years and Champions League participation
- Managerial performance: profitable business (no debt and a capacity to invest)
- Service reliability

This approach relates to the perceived value for the targeted customers in a competitive market. It refers to two other concepts, KSFs and distinctive competence. The KSFs are a necessary condition for success in a given market. They refer to the entirety of the sources of value for the customers in the given sector. Thus, in order to succeed an OSO must identify the sources of value for a particular segment (KSF) in order to deliver this value. Distinctive competence refers to things that an organisation does particularly well, relative to competitors (Selznick, 1957). The relationship between resources, capabilities, and competitive advantage is presented in figure 3.10.

3.4 Strategic Marketing Decisions

The aim of using the method presented in the previous section is to carry out your strategic diagnosis and make it possible for you to collect and summarise significant information. These facts and data allow you to make the following five decisions:

- Which customer segments do you want to satisfy as a priority?
- Which competitive advantage are you going to develop and defend in relation to these segments?
- Which generic strategy are you going to use?
- Which tactics are you going to use?
- Which positioning do you want to adopt?

Target Segment Choice

You must validate your choice of segments using the matrix segment attractiveness versus competitiveness. Thus, OL will concentrate on the following segments: season ticket holders, regular fans, and distant fans. In a complementary mode it will invest resources with a medium-term goal in media switchers and opportunists.

Competing Advantages to Develop Related to the Selected Segments

You must also validate the necessary competitive advantages for the success of your activity in the targeted segments. It is crucial to be pragmatic—that is, you must be sure that the organisation has the resources and capabilities to match these requirements. There is always a gap between existing competitive advantages and ideal ones.

Olympique Lyonnais will allocate resources in order to gain certain competitive advantages in relation to the targeted segments. These are presented in table 3.15.

Figure 3.10 Relationship between resources, capabilities, and competitive advantage.

Table 3.15 OL Competitive Advantages to Develop in Relation to Targeted Fan Segments

	Season ticket holders	Regular fans	Distant fans
Specific competitive advantages	Reliability, good stadium facilities, emotional experience		Responsiveness
	Empathy	None	None
Common competitive advantages	Top sporting results, well managed, international, and user friendly		

Selected Generic Strategy

The club will continue its differentiation strategy because a cost leadership strategy is not relevant in this market, given that fans are willing to spend money when they are involved with the club. This differentiation can be created through management of the following dimensions related to the most important consumer expectations.

Differentiation Related to Intangible Elements

Intangible elements refer to image and the emotional dimension related to your brand. They are powerful elements for differentiation.

Image corresponds to the set of connotations associated with your brand. We presented in a previous chapter a method related to its measurement. Image is a powerful element of differentiation due to the large number of exploitable facets associated with the complexity of human representation and symbolism. Image is influenced by culture, consumption experience, and communication. Image must be managed. To some extent it is a promise to the consumer, and this promise must match with the consumer service experience. For example, if you want to be perceived as user friendly, your service should be responsive and should entail individualised attention to fans. In any case you must determine the image dimensions you wish to reinforce or develop in relation to your targeted fans (see table 3.16 for OL).

We analysed in detail sport experience emotional aspects in the second chapter. This fundamental element allows an OSO to create a durable bond with the people. Consequently, you should define the types of emotions and

Table 3.16 OL Intangible Differentiation Characteristics

Image	Emotions and feelings
• Its president, J.M. Aulas • Competent • Ambitious • Responsible • Sensible	• Pride • Stimulation • Passion • Joy

feelings you want to reinforce or generate for the targeted audience (see table 3.16 for OL).

For Olympique Lyonnais, differentiation by the intangible elements is based on the link between certain managerial values, such as competent, ambitious, responsible, and sensible, and emotions and feelings (e.g., passion, joy, stimulation, and pride). Summing up, it refers to an emotional intelligence. This is a real challenge in this market because many clubs are spending a lot of money for a disappointing sporting result.

Differentiation Related to Tangible Elements

Olympic sport organisations' brand and offer are composed of various elements: core and peripheral services, associated products, staff, facilities, other consumers, and stakeholders. Each one constitutes an axis of differentiation. Nevertheless, these elements are linked together, and it is advisable to find the best combination possible.

Differentiation Related to Core Service and Peripheral Services Differentiation on this dimension can be difficult. It is indeed easy to copy a successful offer related to a segment of customers (strategy of the follower). It is also necessary to invest the relevant resources and competences. In addition, the innovation presents significant risks. No doubt marketers often wonder about the advisability of launching new offers. Indeed, the market, customers' expectations, and competitors' strategies evolve/move, and you cannot remain still. In order to manage this important issue, we recommend the following method.

EXHIBIT 3.4 OFFER INNOVATION PROJECT ANALYSIS

You should consider both existing projects and generation of new projects. For this stage we propose that you build a working group with representatives of the various departments of your organisation. To allow the group to generate new projects, ask them to stress unfulfilled expectations related to consumer segments. They will then need to answer the following questions:

- What did you do in order to improve the service?
- Does this improvement generate new offers?
- If so, why?

Offer innovation can be related to market trends and your competitors. Your working group will need to answer the following questions:

- What are our competitors' new offers?
- What new offers suggested by companies not operating in our market are likely to interest us? Are these offers interesting for us?
- If so, why?
- If not, why?

During this sequence of strategic analysis, you will have to build a matrix combining two criteria: the degree of innovation for the market and the degree of innovation for the organisation (table 3.17). Bréchignac-Roubaud (2000) proposes the following method. To analyse the dimension "innovation for the market", the group will need to answer the question "Why is this offer not on the market?" and give three ideas of criteria. To build the dimension "innovation for the organisation", the group will have to answer the question "What does this offer require of us in addition to our knowledge and of our usual resources?" The group carries out the analysis of the contents of each criterion and draws up a list of criteria.

Once this grid is established for each project, you will ask the group to select a score (going from 1 to 5) for the innovation for the organisation and one relating to the market (figure 3.11).

Table 3.17 Innovation Matrix Criteria

Innovation for the organisation	Innovation for the market
Change in human resources	New expectations fulfilled
Change in facilities and equipment	Offer positioning
Change in operations	Expectation maturity
Experience related to these types of projects	Financial benefits
Resort to subcontractors	Relational benefits
New alliances	

Innovating in the Middle to Long Term

Innovation projects are new for the market and the company. In the long run, innovating projects must be validated by market research, making it possible to verify the existence of these future needs and the relevance for this new offer.

Utility of the Investment?

These projects are not new for the market, but are new for the company. They must be analysed with much care. It is a question of determining if the organisation has the competence and capabilities and if this segment has a sufficient potential.

Growth Potential?

These projects are new for the market and not for the organisation. Nevertheless, you should evaluate the growth potential related to the investment.

Continuous Improvement

These projects are not new, either for the organisation or for the market. Thus they belong in the preceding stage where the question is one of increasing the perceived quality of the service (table 3.18). We developed these aspects previously.

Olympique Lyonnais is not looking for a differentiation based on innovative services. Its strategy is based on the following perceived quality dimensions: reliability, responsiveness, assurance, and empathy. In order to achieve this goal, quality management and staff are essentials.

Differentiation Related to the Staff The staff of an OSO is an essential resource and is part of your offer. It is responsible for service management

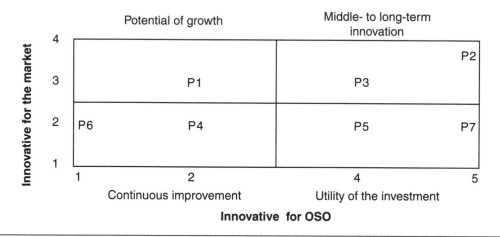

Figure 3.11 Matrix of innovation for the market versus innovation for the organisation.

Table 3.18 Matrix Innovation for the Market Versus Innovation for OL

Potential growth	Middle- to long-term innovation
• Travel agency • Disco	
• Promotional events • Olympique Lyonnais media	• Information through mobile phones (SMS and MMS) • Customised product merchandise • Loyalty card • Licences for merchandised products: "city wear"
Continuous improvement	**Utility of the investment**
Innovative for Olympique Lyonnais	

in relation to the five dimensions of perceived quality. Differentiation through the staff implies recruiting, training, and motivating the staff in order to fulfil the dimensions identified in table 3.19. Olympique Lyonnais is investing in staff in order to fulfil fans' expectations.

Differentiation Related to Facilities   Organisation facilities include buildings, stadium, and equipment. Architectural and internal design allows facilitation of the communication to create or to avoid contacts. It generates positive emotions (relaxation, relief, excitement, etc.) or negative emotions (tension, dissatisfaction, frustration, etc.). Cleanliness is also an important expectation for all the segments. In addition, music, colours, and scents are taken into account in order to generate the right experience.

Although it is an expensive investment, it is important to create a unique and easily recognisable environment in connection with customers' expectations. The stadium is the most important element. The City of Lyon is the owner of Gerland Stadium. The city made a large investment in order to develop the concept of a contemporary urban stadium that is functional and that provides a great emotional experience (table 3.20).

Differentiation Related to Other Consumers and Stakeholders   Consumers and stakeholders are an important issue for an OSO offer. Two aspects can be considered:

- The relationship between customers is directly linked to the desire to develop social relations.
- The sociocultural factor. Some customers are looking for a selective organisation. Others have a greater or lesser tolerance for social diversity.

For soccer club fans, some stakeholders—for example, sponsors, media, and local authorities—are essential. Spectators are an integral part of the event, and in some cases they are the event. Various studies have also shown (Bromberger, Hayot, and Mariottini, 1987;

Table 3.19 **SERVQUAL Perceived Quality Dimensions Related to OSO Staff Competencies**

Dimension	Staff skills and competencies
Tangible aspects	Competence related to expected know-how mastery
Reliability	Capacity to deliver a service in conformance with the promise
Responsiveness	Obligingness and capacity to take consumer problems into fast account
Assurance	Credibility and capacity to be worthy of confidence
Empathy	Capacity to listen to customers' requirements and to communicate with courtesy

Table 3.20 **Gerland Stadium Evolution**

Dates	Characteristics
1913	A Greco-Roman-style stadium designed to organise bicycle races, track and field competitions, processions, popular events, and school festivals. Capacity: 30,000 seats
1950s to 1984 (European Championship)	• Redesigned for cycling, track and field, and football • Removal of the athletics and cycle-racing tracks • Roofing of the two side stands, which provided a stadium in rectangular form, breaking with the traditional circular form
1998 (World Cup)	• Complete renovation and redesign (cost: 33 M euros, more than 50% by the town of Lyon). Capacity: 41,051 seats

Bromberger, 1995, 1997, 1999; Lanfranchi, 1996) that characteristics, needs, and fan behaviour differ widely within a stadium and throughout European stadiums. Despite various differences, OL's social base characteristics are close to those of the Red and Blue fan group (see table 3.21).

Tactics Related to Competitors

Olympique Lyonnais should maintain its actual tactics, that is, as leader at a French level and challenger at a European level. Success is related to sporting results, which depend on the sport sector. Marketing will bring new financial resources by exploiting new products and alliances in order to hit each targeted segment. It will help to reposition the OL brand.

Positioning

Positioning is determined by consumer perception. Positioning is also a process aimed at creating an image for a brand in the minds of target customers, and OSO strategists do not have total control over it. Consequently there is an interaction between the target audience representation and OSO marketing efforts. Figure 3.12 presents these interactions and the possible gaps.

In the previous section, we presented a method for diagnosing OSO brand positioning. Planning positioning requires a process including the following steps (Dibb, 2000):

- Step 1. Define the segments in the marketplace under consideration.

- Step 2. Decide which segment or combination of segments to target.

- Step 3. Develop a clear understanding of the expectations of target consumers.

- Step 4. Ensure that the offer matches the expectations identified.

- Step 5. Evaluate brand image and positioning and the images, as perceived by the targeted customers, of competing products in the selected market segment or segments.

Table 3.21 Five Groups of OL Fans

Name	Characteristics
Bad Gones	The oldest and the most significant group of Olympique Lyonnais fans. Founded in 1987, when the club was in the second division. About 2,500 members are located in the northern stand. They are slightly aggressive and intolerant. Motto: To fight and to win Web site: www.bg87.com
Lugdunums	Like Bad Gones, they affiliate with the extremist movement. Founded in 1993; 1,000 members. Lugdunums are located in the southern lower stand. Motto: "Lyon et basta" Web site: www.lugdu1993.com
Red and Blue	Founded in May 2000, with 200 members, the Red and Blue are a more gentle group, offering a family subscription and aiming at exemplary behaviour. Their rules: "To be positive in respect to the club, whatever the situation"; "to treat unfavourable clubs and referees with courtesy, respect, and tolerance"; and "not to tolerate violence and vulgarity in the stands" Motto: Together to win Web site: www.lesrougeetbleu.com
Nucleo Ultra	Founded in 2000, they are located in the south stand; 70 members. Motto: We are Lyons, We are atypical Web site: nucleolyon.free.fr
Hex@gones	Founded in December 2000, they are located in all stands except the northern one; 155 members. Motto: Lyonnais from here or elsewhere, proud of our colours Web site: www.hexagones.org

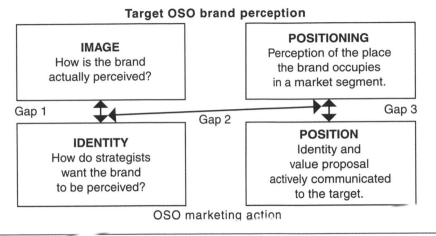

Target OSO brand perception

IMAGE
How is the brand
actually perceived?

POSITIONING
Perception of the place
the brand occupies
in a market segment.

Gap 1   Gap 2   Gap 3

IDENTITY
How do strategists
want the brand
to be perceived?

POSITION
Identity and
value proposal
actively communicated
to the target.

OSO marketing action

Figure 3.12 Relations between image and positioning and between identity and position.

- Step 6. Select an image that sets the brand apart from the competing brands, thus ensuring that the chosen image matches the aspirations of the target consumer.
- Step 7. Inform target consumers about the product.

There are four types of positioning (step 6) in relation to the benefits presented in the previous chapter (see discussion of experiential value promise in chapter 2).

1. Functional positioning related to cognitive benefits (rational)
2. Psychological positioning providing personal achievement, self-expression, self-image enhancement, mental stimulation, and affective fulfilment
3. Sociocultural positioning, referring to values, belongingness, and social meaningfulness
4. Experiential positioning providing sensory and cognitive benefits

Olympique Lyonnais uses an experiential positioning associating sport and managerial performance with sociocultural factors. We stressed the fact that club managers intend to develop a differentiation mixing managerial values such as competent, ambitious, responsible, and sensible in connection with emotions and feelings like passion, joy, stimulation, and pride. The OL positioning statement synthesises these aspects.

A positioning statement facilitates communication to the target. It is simply a formal statement depicting how you want your target segment to perceive you. In essence, then, it is a promise to the target segment that you will provide them with the benefits they care about the most. The positioning statement is less an external marketing tactic and more an internal document that helps the firm direct its marketing efforts.

A positioning statement has four parts: the name of the customer segment, the most important benefits to that segment, the primary competitors (this is not all that important, however), and the key reasons why you can provide the customer benefits better than the competition. It can be written in the form of answers to the following questions.

- For whom? Aim at specifying the target characteristics and their main expectations. Olympique Lyonnais is a French club for all soccer fans eager to be impassioned about a well-managed performing European club.
- What? Specify the market for the offer, for example, French and European soccer.
- Why? Express the reasons people will prefer this brand rather than those of the competition. Thus, OL is the winner of three consecutive French Championships and a two-time UEFA Champions League quarter-finalist. It has an efficient management led by a sensible and competent president, Jean-Michel Aulas. It has a long history and tradition. It is an authentic user-friendly club. Olympique Lyonnais does care about its fans.

The most difficult part of writing a positioning statement is identifying the key reasons for differentiation from competitors. This information, of course, comes from the organisation analysis. The question to ask is why your company can promise these benefits better than the competition. You cannot talk about just any competencies or strengths, but rather only those strengths that directly relate to the benefits desired by the customer segment. This is the essence of finding a differential advantage over the competition.

3.5 Conclusion

The strategic stage is usually the decisive one. Despite its importance, the nature and role of strategy for OSOs is often rather vague and incompletely specified. Chappelet's (2004) contribution aims at specifying how strategic management concepts and methods can be applied to entities within the Olympic system. The purpose of this chapter was to present a method based on common principles and to translate that into practical implications for marketing strategy, illustrated with the case of the professional soccer club Olympique Lyonnais.

Strategy is an ongoing process aimed at getting into an attractive position in your marketplace and developing resources and competences superior to those of the competitors. An offering will not build values unless these two requirements are simultaneously met. According to Marthur (2000), these act as scissor blades. One blade refers to an attractive market position, the other to winning resources. The combination of the two adds value to the offering.

We develop five strategic marketing decisions aimed at getting into an attractive market position:

- Targeting customer segments
- Selecting competitive advantage to develop and defend in relation to these segments

- Choosing a generic strategy
- Choosing a tactic
- Choosing a relevant positioning

Winning resources refers to human and financial resources. We noted that there is often a gap between organisation culture and the plan. Human resources management stresses the importance of staff involvement in the implementation of strategy. In this context internal marketing is an important implementation tool. It aids communication and helps us to overcome any resistance to change. It informs all staff and involves them in new initiatives and strategies. This can be achieved through communication, a refinement of the common practices through progressive group work that allows members to succeed together. To reach this expertise, each organisation unit should evolve according to five stages.

- The stage of latency in which the group is an agglomerate of people functioning in a partitioned way and not having any team direction
- The stage of membership in which there is a feeling of community, but not of engagement towards a shared objective
- The team stage, characterised by a common objective and a beginning of collective practices
- The stage of joint action, in which collective operation supersedes individual operation
- The stage of collective intelligence, in which the group has the capacity to find solutions making it possible to adapt to react to a threat or to benefit from an opportunity

Furthermore, to achieve this purpose at the OSO level it is necessary to ensure the interaction of departments and units.

four

Managing an Olympic Sport Organisation's Sponsorship

During the last 30 last years, sponsorship has advanced significantly at both the strategic level and the operational level. We can distinguish three periods. The 1980s are remembered for the fast development of events supported by an increasing presence in the media. Many companies were involved in sponsorship in order to dissociate from traditional modes of communication, to develop a relationship with their communication target, to develop their public image, and to increase awareness. All sporting organisations—federations, clubs, event organisers—set themselves up to find partners. However, after a phase of enthusiasm, the decision makers raised questions concerning the selection and effectiveness of these operations. Sponsoring was then used as a means of communication and they worked in order to integrate it into their communication strategy.

During the following decade, companies sought to link their strategy of sponsoring with other variables of their action marketing while being organised in order to obtain a better return on investment. In addition, the entities involved were organised to fight against the strategies of ambush marketing, or parasitic marketing, that emerged in the middle of the 1980s. Currently the question is one of integrating sponsorship into the various strategies of the company and of developing synergies between them. We have entered the era of activation of the sponsor's brand with the various targets of the company. Activation is a marketing strategy aimed at giving the people concerned a positive experience with the sponsor's brand in relation to the event.

Despite this long experience, developing a profitable, sustainable sponsorship programme still raises a certain number of questions:

- What exactly is sponsoring?
- How does it work?
- What mechanisms does it require?
- Does sponsoring have a link to theories of persuasive communication?

In this chapter we present a new operational approach aimed at helping both sponsors and sponsees to make the right strategic choices and guarantee the success of sponsoring programmes. For this purpose, we provide a theoretical basis for your sponsoring activities by presenting concepts, methods, and tools. This approach will be illustrated with the case of the Slovenian National Olympic Committee.

EXHIBIT 4.1 THE SLOVENIAN OLYMPIC COMMITTEE

The Slovenian Olympic Committee (SOC; official name is National Olympic Committee of Slovenia) was founded in 1991 and recognised by the IOC in 1992. It merged with the former Association of Sports Federations (ASF) of Slovenia into one consolidated organisation in December 1994. The Sports Association of Slovenia (set up in 1945), an umbrella organisation of national sport federations in Slovenia, merged with the Olympic Committee of Slovenia (OCS) in December 1994 to become the OCS-ASF, which has since represented the majority of organised sport in Slovenia. In accordance with the umbrella organisation's tasks, the OCS-ASF represents the interests of its members. The SOC–Association of Sports Federations (OCS-ASF) operates as an umbrella sport organisation, comprising almost all national sport federations in Slovenia.

The OCS-ASF cooperates with various international institutions, primarily those actively involved in the Olympic movement (IOC, ANOC, EOC, IFs, NOCs, ICAS, AGFIS, ENGSO, WADA, WHO, EU, Council of Europe) according to the international relations strategy respecting the OCS statutes submitted by its Commission for International Relations and approved by its executive board.

The NOC of Slovenia Top Sports Committee's responsibilities are, in coordination with the NFs, organisation of multisport projects; categorisation system for Slovenian athletes; system of scholarships for promising young athletes; health insurance and medical assistance for top sport athletes; licensing of private sport workers; organisation of technical seminars for sport experts and officials; data processing; activities related to foundation; and assistance in the work of the National Anti-Doping Commission, NOC athletes' commission, and Club of the Slovenian Olympians. The National Anti-Doping Commission was founded jointly by the Ministry of Education, Science and Sport and the NOC of Slovenia–Association of Sports Federations.

The Olympic Games are of the utmost importance to the NOC of Slovenia. For each Olympic Games, a special project is carried out. The key to success is excellent coordination and cooperation with the national sport federations. In fact, all the decisions, or at least all the most important decisions, are made in accordance with the NFs.

In coordination with the NF, the NOC of Slovenia is responsible for the following multisport projects: Olympic Games, Mediterranean Games, EYOF, ALPE ADRIA, Youth Games, the Three Countries Youth Games.

The Sport for All Committee, in coordination with governing and nongoverning Sport for All organisations (sport clubs; NFs; Faculty of Sport; Institute for Sport of the Republic of Slovenia; Ministry of Education, Science and Sport; Slovenian elementary and secondary schools), is mainly responsible for the organisation of the following projects: Slovenian Olympic Card, Olympic Day Runs, Slovenia Runs and Cycles, Slovenian Congress of Sports Recreation, Prescription for Healthy Life with Sport, Football Street.

The Commune Level Sport Committee priorities are cooperation with volunteers on local levels and creation of central regional sport offices in Slovenia. The central regional offices will be located in Maribor, Moravske toplice, Kranj, and Koper, with renovation of several sport centres such as the Planica ski flying hill, Bezigrad Football Stadium, and Bonifica Sports Centre in Koper.

The Women in Sport Commission was founded in 2003.

The Slovenian Olympic Academy operates within the NOC of Slovenia–Association of Sports Federations as its body responsible for concern for fair play and tolerance and orientation towards awareness of the general public about the values of Olympism and sport in general. The first and foremost concern of the Slovenian Olympic Academy and the Ambassador for Sport, Tolerance and Fair Play of the Republic of Slovenia is to put the programme of the Slovenian Academy into practice so that it is experienced by all those target groups the Olympic ideal is meant for. Projects include a children's drawing contest organised in Slovenian schools, a project aimed at presenting children's awareness of various sports; "one Hour of Olympism and Fair Play Movement in the Slovenian Elementary Schools", dedicated to Olympic ideas, sports, values, and principles; publications on Olympism and sports; photo contests; organisation of seminars and educational programmes for trainers, judges, and referees; and discussions with members of the national football team about fair play, tolerance, and doping. Workshops ("Sports Protocol—Positive and Creative Communication in English") are being organised for young athletes and for Slovene English-speaking contact persons of national sport organisations, providing training in communication skills and how to avoid conflicts arising from intercultural and linguistic differences.

The key governance principles to be respected by all members of the sport organisations are transparency, fairness, equity, and democracy. Under the by-laws of the OCS statutes, fines and other disciplinary measures can be taken against a member federation that does not abide by good governance principles, although these have been rarely put into practice so far. However, given the state's funding guidelines and the sport movement's self-regulation of various aspects of good governance, some Slovenian sport federations have expressed their wish to get expert support from the NOC of Slovenia–Association of Sports Federations before taking legal steps to enforce these principles with their constituency. The procedure for establishment of the Court of Arbitration for Sport has already begun and is expected to be completed in the near future.

4.1 Defining Sponsoring

Meenaghan (1998) comments that the perception of sponsoring has changed, not only for sponsors but also for owners of events and for consumers. Managing sponsoring has also evolved. The combination of these two factors explains why today, no definition is unanimously accepted. As a first stage, we shall analyse the main definitions that have been proposed since the beginning of the 1980s. Secondly, we shall identify the discriminating criteria of this technique in order to propose an operational definition in today's context.

Some Definitions of Sponsoring

According to Sahnoun (1986), "Sponsorship is a communication tool that makes it possible, for a given public, to link a brand or a firm directly with an attractive event". This definition underlines one of the essential points of sponsoring, that is, the direct link between a sponsor and an event. Sponsoring is seen as a technique for communication aimed at reaching the target group made up of the public interested in the event. We shall see that this conception restricts the strategic possibilities concerning the use of sponsoring. Sponsoring must be integrated into the marketing strategy in order to establish synergies between a certain number of variables within the mix.

This link between marketing strategy and sponsoring appeared later. Sandler and Shani

(1989) consider sponsoring to consist of resources (such as money, human and material resources) that are supplied by an organisation directly to an event or to an activity in exchange for a direct association with this event or activity. The organisation supplying these resources can then use this direct association in order to achieve institutional, marketing, or media coverage objectives. This definition presents the objectives of sponsoring as having a marketing or institutional nature (or a combination of the two). In this case, the question is one of contributing towards integrating the citizen company within its environment and of conferring upon it the status of an institution, improving the perception of its mission and its role. Two other important points emanate from this definition. On the one hand, sponsoring is part of a process of exchange between a sponsor company and an organisation (sport or other); on the other, it is a commercial agreement between the holder of rights and the company that makes it possible to exploit this direct association in order to attain objectives.

At the beginning of the 1990s, companies used sponsoring more and more for commercial purposes. This was favoured by a slowing of the economy that began in 1991. Meenaghan (1991) expressed this tendency by suggesting that "sponsorship is an investment, in cash or in kind, in an activity, in return for access to the exploitable commercial potential associated with that activity". Crowley (1991), Javalgi et al. (1994), and McDonald (1991) confirm this approach. Several years later, Grey and Skildum-Reid (1999) situated themselves in the same perspective and defined the diversity of the entities that can serve as support to sponsoring: "Sponsorship is an investment in sport, the arts, a community event, individual, venue, broadcast, institution, program or cause which yields a commercial return for the sponsor". However, over the last decade a wider direction to sponsoring has also developed, one that can be termed a "business-exchange relationship" (Irwin and Sutton, 1994; Ferrand and Pagès, 1996).

According to Derbaix, Gérard, and Lardinois (1994) "Sponsorship is a technique that, for all organisations, consists of creating or discreetly supporting a sociocultural event that is independent as such, and becoming associated with it from a media point of view with a view to achieving marketing objectives".

An Operational Definition of Sponsoring

During the early years of this century, a certain number of principles that became clear from the preceding definitions have remained valid. Since sponsoring is an evolutionary strategy, it is necessary to bring the definition up to date. Without claiming to be exhaustive, we propose the following definition.

Sponsoring is a persuasive communication strategy integrated within marketing that pursues commercial or institutional objectives, exploiting the direct association between an organisation, a brand, or a product with another organisation, brand, or personality and implying a commercial transaction between the various parties concerned.

Sponsoring presents two forms that can be combined: "on-site" sponsoring and "media sponsorship". We shall now develop each term within this definition.

Sponsoring As a Communication Strategy Integrated Within Marketing

The sponsoring company implements a series of strategies that function on the principle of integration. These are presented in the diagram of figure 4.1. The strategy corresponds to all choices made in the medium and long term by the company, given its view of the environment and the potential that this presents. These choices or strategic decisions refer to the nature and extent of the means the company envisages using in order to carry out a coordinated action in the market. The strategy concerning the market refers to the variables of the marketing action. It uses functional policies plus human and financial resources, research and development, and production.

The integration of sponsoring within communication strategy is increasingly well mastered. According to Brochand and Lendrevie (2000), communication strategy is "all major and interdependent decisions regarding objectives to be achieved and the main resources to be implemented in order to fulfil them". Sponsoring thus constitutes one of the means of communication that a company can use in order to achieve a certain number of objectives such as increased

awareness, positioning of image, reinforcing relations with clients (figure 4.1).

If the integration of sponsoring strategy within communication strategy was one of the major issues at stake during the 1990s, the integration of communication strategy into marketing strategy is the issue for the new decade. The integration of communication with marketing constitutes a substantial competitive advantage for organisations. The use of the term integrated marketing communication (IMC) expresses this desire. According to Shimp (1997), this constitutes "the process of developing and implementing persuasive communications programmes planned to target consumers and prospects. The objective of IMC is to influence or to act directly on the behaviour of selected communication targets. For a company, IMC takes into account all sources of contact between the brand or a company that a consumer possesses with the product or service as a vector for communicating future messages. IMC uses all forms of communication appropriate to the consumer and to prospects and that can be assimilated". Integrated marketing communication thus presents the following characteristics:

1. Its objective is to influence the behaviour of the target.

2. It uses all forms of contact between the company and the target.

3. It begins with the consumer or the prospect, which implies knowing the consumer well.

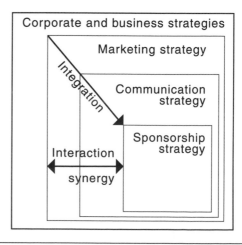

Figure 4.1 Integration and interaction of sponsoring with various strategies of the company.

4. It accomplishes a synergy between the various communication tools and between the communications strategy and the other variables within the marketing action.

5. It constructs relations between the company and its clients, its suppliers, and its distribution network.

Strategic management of sponsoring takes all these characteristics into account. We shall integrate them within an operational approach.

Sponsoring is not only integrated within various strategies; it interacts and establishes synergies with them. In fact, a sponsoring operation interacts with the marketing strategy when it stimulates the sales force and the distribution network, when it makes it possible to conceive a new service (sport results on your mobile phone), or when it provides support for a promotion. A sponsoring operation also functions in synergy with global strategy when it stimulates partnership with the institutional networks in a country in order to favour the company's globalisation.

The example of the sponsors of the "Top programme" at the level of the Olympic Games in 1996 also expresses a certain number of synergies. According to the study by Ludwig and Karabetsos (1999), the objectives, in order of importance, were these:

1. Obtaining exclusivity in the product category
2. Increasing awareness
3. Increasing sales
4. Creating or changing an image
5. Obtaining impact via the media
6. Seizing a unique opportunity for offering hospitality
7. Increasing market share
8. Reaching specific market segments
9. Showing goodwill (value)
10. Reinforcing relations among employees
11. Following Olympic tradition

Synergies appear on a level of overall strategy and marketing strategy when it is a question of increasing sales and market share or achieving specific market segments. They also concern internal communication when the aim is to reinforce relations among employees.

Pursuing Commercial or Institutional Objectives

We have stressed, in this section, that it is possible to group together sponsoring objectives in two categories: commercial communication and corporate communication. We shall situate the major objectives of sponsoring in these two dimensions.

Sponsorship and Commercial Communication Several sponsoring strategies exist. Depending on the objectives sought, these can be implemented individually or in combination. The following subsections present a breakdown.

Sponsoring to Promote Credibility Historically, gaining credibility was the first objective assigned to sponsoring. Through involvement in an event, the company seeks to demonstrate the technical performance of its products and services. These can intervene directly or indirectly in the event. Traditionally, these sponsors enter into the category of official suppliers. Sponsoring serves the product policy of these companies, which usually work in the technical or technology sectors.

This technique is well used by the Swiss watchmaker concern, the Swatch Group, via their company Swiss Timing. In exchange for its timing services, the group obtains visibility for its brands, depending on the sports covered, relating to the positioning of these brands and their target publics: for example, Tissot and cycling, Omega and golf, and Longines and gymnastics.

IBM has long used encrusted logos when providing ranking and results lists on television broadcasts for the Olympic Games, revealing to the entire world the quality of its products and its information technology services.

Automobile manufacturers invest massively in Formula 1 racing in order to anchor their image and demonstrate their know-how in research and development, and then communicate this association to consumers who drive cars and who attach a great deal of importance to technology, performance, and security.

Certain equipment suppliers and ball suppliers use this strategy to anchor their domination in the market—for example, Mikasa, which provides the official ball used for volleyball and water polo.

Sponsoring to Increase Awareness Awareness corresponds to familiarity, diffusion of the knowledge of a brand or of a product within a population. In the strict sense, awareness corresponds to being recognised or referred to independently of the qualitative components of the image (Serraf, 1985). There are two types of awareness that are closely correlated. Unprompted awareness corresponds to the percentage of individuals capable of spontaneously citing a brand or an event within the universe of the product concerned. This indicator evaluates memorisation. "Top of mind" corresponds to the brand most often cited in first position. Prompted awareness is expressed as the percentage of individuals capable of citing the brand or the event within a list on which they are featured. This indicator makes it possible to assess the capacity to recognise the various brands. The number of individuals with this type of awareness is usually higher than for spontaneous awareness.

PDM, a manufacturer of videocassettes, decided to sponsor a team of cyclists taking part in the Tour de France, and in one month succeeded in achieving tremendous awareness in its targeted market, western Europe.

Z, a chain of stores for children's goods, followed the same strategy and succeeded in seeing its number of shops and its turnover soar thanks to increased awareness after Greg LeMond won the Tour de France wearing the chain's colours.

Amstel beer invested massively in the UEFA Champions League for football in order to increase awareness among European consumers. The results in terms of awareness, consumption, and penetration in beverage stands were excellent in all markets targeted. This was attributable to numerous special activities such as a fan hat competition, which provided exceptional additional media visibility and an association with moments of emotion and friendship among fans.

Sponsoring Focused on Image We have defined the term "image" in a previous chapter, and stated that image is a mental representation of an entity that can be assimilated with the cog-

nitive component of attitude. In the context of sponsoring focused on image, the sponsor seeks to appropriate, for itself, for one of its brands or products, the image of a sport event. This "appropriation" can call upon two mechanisms that we analyse in detail in this section. The first consists of reinforcing the image traits that the sponsor shares with the object receiving sponsorship. The second consists of transferring the specific image traits belonging to the sponsored object to the image of the sponsor.

We have seen that image is an essential component of brand capital. Managing it is thus important from a strategic point of view. Figure 4.2 illustrates image management within the framework of a sponsoring operation; we shall present its internal dynamic.

The base of the triangle concerns the link between the image of the sponsor and the identity it wishes to communicate actively to the target. If the two correspond, this situation will be reinforced. If this is not so, it will be necessary to modify the present image (displacement strategy).

Once the strategy is established, the company is in a position to evaluate each possibility for sponsorship. This diagnostic evaluation makes it possible to analyse existing links between its image and that of the event (or more generally

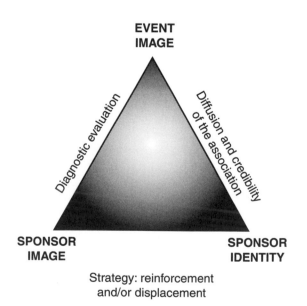

Figure 4.2 Strategic diagnostic referring to identity and image (Ferrand and Pagès, 1996).

of the object to be sponsored). It is thus possible to pinpoint common traits and those specific to each entity in order to choose a reinforcement or a displacement strategy.

The third side of the triangle concerns the diffusion of the association between the image of the event and the identity that the sponsor wishes to communicate. If brand X sponsors event Y because it wishes to transfer the notion of conviviality, the public concerned will emit a judgement that is both emotional (I accept this or I don't) and rational (I find this brand more convivial or I don't). This is an essential point that a company must evaluate before taking any decision to provide sponsorship.

Creating Dynamism for the Distribution Network
Any sponsoring operation can make it possible to create a direct, emotional link plus increased dynamism within a distribution network by associating with it, directly or indirectly. This is the case for Peugeot as sponsor to Roland Garros when, together with its outlets, it organises Peugeot/Roland Garros days, a series of tournaments organised in France and reserved for clients of these outlets. This type of operation also reinforces partnership links.

Stimulating the Sales Force (Sponsoring Based on Emulation)
A company can also use an event as a basis to stimulate the sales force in order to obtain better commercial results. This can take the form of an "incentive" when the company chooses to reward its best sales staff by inviting them to the Roland Garros tennis tournament. The company can also benefit from interest in the event on the part of the clientele in order to produce additional arguments for sales staff with a view to increasing sales: activities in outlets, publicity at the point of sale, games and competitions, and so on.

Generating Goodwill and Positive Attitude
Another sponsorship strategy aims at generating a feeling of goodwill and a positive attitude towards the sponsor's brand. These positive feelings occur when sponsor involvement contributes to the development of sport or to the organisation of an event. So, in the context of the Olympic Games of Atlanta, 87% of the audience expressed their agreement with the proposal that "sponsoring contributes largely to the success of the Olympics Games", and 55% of them expressed a positive attitude towards official sponsors.

Increasing Sales
In some specific situations and targets, sponsorship could stimulate sales. Examples such as the operation of Banesto, sponsor of a cyclist team during the Vuelta in Spain, demonstrate that combined with a promotional operation delivering some tangible benefit to the consumer, sponsoring can have an immediate effect on the sales and that it is advisable to use strategies in combination to increase the sales.

Developing Business-to-Business Relationships
Hospitality during the event remains the best means to develop business relationships. Guests can enjoy themselves in a prestigious and controlled environment allowing the creation of personal contacts. The majority of event sponsorship packages include this type of service. It is crucial to be aware that the event must be attractive to these company executives and managers. Furthermore, the environment must combine social selectivity with a pleasant and memorable experience. This offer is one of the competitive advantages of event sponsorship.

Thus, Schweppes used the possibilities of hospitality of Formula 1 team West McLaren Mercedes to develop contacts with key persons in charge of purchase and distribution. Sometimes these VIP hospitality packages allow the sponsor to present its products. British Telecom used BT Total Challenge and the Rugby World Cup to exhibit its products and technologies used within the framework of the event.

Sponsorship and Corporate Communication
Corporate strategies aim to communicate certain fundamental societal values held by companies via sport. They make it possible to allay some negative perceptions that public opinion may have of these companies, who seek to restore their image in this way. By promoting their image in general and their ecological or social image in particular through such programmes, companies promote themselves. Certain industries that are considered indispensable but that create pollution have little else but such strategies for communicating, in a credible way, beyond their actual activities. Such strategies also make it possible to

communicate the economic performance of companies that use them.

Company financial performance can also involve negative reactions. An involvement towards social causes can enable a company to show that it takes into account the human dimension and that it is able to redistribute a part of its benefits. Thus, by developing their image and their ecological or social engagement, these organisations develop their companies through these programmes. These strategies also make it possible to communicate in connection with the firm's economic performance. Four categories of objectives enter into the framework of institutional communication.

Reassuring Actors in the Financial World Sponsorship can aim at developing relations with key actors of the financial world in order to reassure them. It is possible to use hospitality programmes and public relations in the context of a financial communication. Thus, Ballantine's invited a group of financial analysts to Urban High, a sponsored event in Spain. According to the management of the company, this operation had a direct effect on stock exchange valorisation of £280 million.

Proving Citizenship and Legitimating Company Social Performance After the 1960s, companies became aware that their harmonious integration in the local community contributes to establishing good relations with people and institutional actors. Furthermore, it has a positive influence on internal climate, reducing conflicts. The company is no longer a closed space, but an actor open to the environment. Sponsorship aims at demonstrating firm social concerns and commitment. It thus seeks to develop the firm's relationships to the community.

Sponsorship constitutes an excellent vector of integration in the local community. For example, Packard Bell, in collaboration with the city of Leeds and Leeds United, for which it was the sponsor, was involved in an educational programme aimed at developing qualified data processing among underprivileged children. This is another competitive advantage of sport sponsorship, extensively used by local events and clubs, that makes it possible for sponsors to be anchored in the local life and the territory.

Promoting Company Culture, Reinforcing Internal Cohesion, and Motivating Staff Staff is an essential component of a company. Successful companies are those that not only have the means to recruit qualified people, but also can create a common culture directed towards the satisfaction of the customer, develop cohesion between people, and support their development. A football team illustrates this principle. It is not enough to buy the best players to win the UEFA Champions League. It is necessary to be able to involve them and to make them play together.

Sport sponsorship provides a very interesting platform for creating social bonds. For example, a local basketball club might seek a company partner for each game. The company invites all the personnel and their families. People can meet the executives and leaders, who are also with their families. The children may meet the players after the match. Players organise training sessions and games. This initiative has a positive effect on the motivation of the personnel and the working relationships.

Improving Staff Recruitment Quality staff recruitment constitutes another key factor because it directly influences firm performance. From this point of view, the company must develop its attractiveness, in particular though its corporate image. Sport sponsorship can contribute to this goal. Thus, ECCO (a staffing and human resources company) used its commitment as a sponsor of the Rock Climbing Master Series at the end of the 1980s to recruit qualified staff, communicating the theme of the mutual assistance and confidence that link two members of a rope. A petrol company, ELF, used this strategy in a broader dimension related to human resource management. This company was facing several problems:

- Significantly heavy staff workload
- Significant requests for new employees
- Difficulty attracting qualified personnel
- Significant staff turnover
- Weak staff involvement
- Feeling of isolation in regional branches

The company became involved as a Whitbread sponsor in order to use the event to improve internal communication, increase staff involvement, and recruit qualified personnel.

Exploiting the Association With Another Organisation, Event, or Personality

Direct association constitutes one of the basic principles of sponsoring. Figure 4.3 allows one to situate the various possibilities for association that exist between the sponsor and the entity receiving sponsoring. The many choices represent several questions for the strategic core of the company.

- Should we be associated with an event, a team, a sport organisation?
- What sort of sponsoring management do we need to avoid any cannibalism on the part of another sponsor?
- How do we protect ourselves against ambush marketing operations?

No Powerful Social Impact Without an Event The dynamics of this system are mainly guaranteed by the event. Events generate a social impact; and the sport organisation, the teams, and the athletes all benefit from the power of sport events. In fact, what would the impact of the best tennis player be if there were no ATP tournaments? We shall therefore define the concept of an event and analyse the reasons for this impact.

The Sport Event As a Social Factor The term "event" comes from the Latin "eventus" meaning "what has come"—something whose arrival affects an individual or a human community to some extent. Piquet (1985) used this conception as a basis when considering that "an event is above all a strong social factor, a place where men and women gather in a sort of collective celebration to attend a sport or cultural type of entertainment. This is subjectively perceived as the possibility of achieving an exploit".

The event has a sociocultural anchor that possesses its own identity. For this reason, it must be understood as a social factor in the sense described by Durkheim (1894), for whom it is "any way of doing something, fixed or not, and likely to exert an external constraint on the individual, or even what is general within a given society while having its own existence independent of its individual manifestations". The particular social factors that are sport "shows" were notably studied by Bourdieu (1979), Pociello (1983), and Bromberger, Hayot, and Mariottini (1987). These latter analysed sport entertainment as an object of relative consensus but above all as a support for differentiation and a vehicle for values and social representations. Moreover, the differentiated properties portrayed by a sport show appear to predispose each group of spectators to make a specific investment. In fact, within the stadium, individuals divide themselves up according to a combination of criteria; contrasting sociological universes emerge, and specific social identities are confirmed.

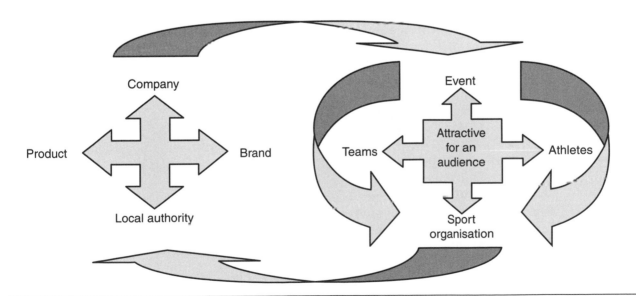

Figure 4.3 The many possible types of association within the framework of sponsoring.

Social Sharing of Emotions in the Event Emotion is at the heart of the event. According to Maffesoli (1988), "Common sensitivity . . . comes from the fact of taking part, or corresponds, in the strongest and perhaps mystical sense of these terms, to a common ethos". Thus, that which is favoured is less what one will voluntarily adhere to (contractual, mechanical perspective) and more what is emotionally common to all (sensitive, organic perspective). This is therefore a fundamental mechanism by which the sport event produces an identitarian experience within what can be called "affectual communities" (Maffesoli, 1988). We should underline the essential role of intervention in a socially shared mode of expression. Television, like the media in the wider sense, makes it possible to create virtual communities. In a society that is more and more dominated by communication, these communities offer new support for participation by individuals in relational, social life.

A Common Symbolic Space The mobilisation of the emotional aspect within these communities takes place within specific, symbolic spaces. Bromberger, Hayot, and Mariottini's (1987) ethnological analysis of the popular enthusiasm for the football clubs of Marseilles and Turin and their matches takes into account the relations between what is symbolic and what is affective. These authors thus ask themselves "according to which mechanisms, which types of mediation, are these properties of the game, the show, the competition the object of symbolic and emotional commitment". Football is of course an "exceptional melting pot for identification" in which the team constitutes the symbol of collective identity. This social backdrop offers a multitude of possibilities for identification that are valorised within the cultural universe of the spectators. These are essentially values linked to surpassing oneself and performance. Their cultural anchor goes back a long way, as far as ancient Greece. According to Huizinga (1951), "In the interest shown by the public for sporting exploits, there is recognition of the values of individual force, the desire for power, courage associated with struggle, rivalry or victory".

This symbolic potential unique to sport could hardly fail to interest companies. Semiology is also interested in sport as a show. According to Barthes (1957), sport is "a genuine human comedy, where the social nuances of passion (conceit, rightfulness, refined cruelty, sense of 'paying one's debts'), fortunately also find the clearest sign that can gather them up, express them and bear them triumphantly to the interior of the stadium". Gritti (1975) considers that the extent of sporting vocabulary goes well beyond the framework of sport: "The blossoming wealth of terms, the many-coloured spectrum of lively colours unfurl an incomparable anthology of vocabulary, images, motivations, lifestyles that work naturally within sports rhetoric, meaning they are profoundly shared by the various and varied publics at major sports events".

Implying a Commercial Transaction Between Parties

When finalised, a commercial transaction gives rise to a contract's being drawn up. This notion leads to two aspects. The first relates to the exchange process that, for the sponsor or owner of the event, means obtaining something in return for something else. In the area of sponsoring, this can mean exchanging money or services in return for displaying the logo at the event or elsewhere. Kotler, Dubois, and Manceau (2003) suggest that the four following conditions must be satisfied in order for exchange to take place:

- Two parties exist.
- Each party possesses something that can be of value to the other.
- Both parties are able to communicate and deliver what is exchanged.
- Each party is free to accept or refuse the other's offer.

If both parties are interested, they will seek to reach agreement on the terms of the exchange. If agreement is reached, this will lead to a transaction (monetary, material, service, etc.). This transaction is formalised by a contract. The contract is subject to commercial law and includes an agreement on what will be exchanged, the terms, and the time and the place of exchange. Since sponsoring requires action in the medium to long term, we can speak of establishing a relationship between the two parties (figure 4.4).

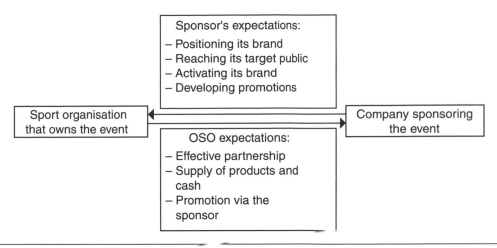

Figure 4.4 The exchange between two entities with indication of their expectations.

Control and Protection of the Event's Brand Derbaix, Gérard, and Lardinois (1994) point out that sponsorship can't be successful if the right owner is not controlling the event. In this context, the event rights owner must protect it like a brand.[1] The recipient of sponsoring must therefore be assured, in advance, that it can really deliver the rights promised to the sponsor. The development of its inventory and the offers that it will make take into account only benefits that can be delivered to sponsors. It is on this point that most conflicts arise, and it is for this reason that contracts for sponsoring are often necessary.

Sponsorship and Ambush Marketing Ambush marketing is a strategy linked to efforts by an organisation to become indirectly associated with an event, to attempt to obtain the same benefits as an official sponsor without paying the official royalties to whoever holds the rights. In fact, most types of partnership are concluded on the basis of exclusivity for categories of products. For example, since Coca-Cola was a sponsor of the Football World Cup, Pepsi could not benefit from an official partnership. However, in order to be present nevertheless and to communicate to target consumers, Pepsi invested massively in television commercials of a humorous nature, portraying Sumo wrestlers (the World Cup took place in Japan and South Korea) ridiculing themselves in a football match. Since the commercials were chosen to be shown around repeat broadcasts of matches, confusion could take place in the minds of consumers regarding who really was the sponsor of the event and which sponsor produced the greatest emotional and cognitive impact.

Examples of ambush marketing in sport are sadly innumerable, from extremely well-organised campaigns to banners placed surreptitiously within camera ranges. It is the responsibility of those holding the rights to ensure that the rights of official sponsors are respected. The IOC deploys huge efforts to track down "cheats" at the Olympic Games in every corner of the globe.

It is worth adding that in the example just cited, it is difficult to accuse Pepsi of ambush marketing because it is perfectly legal to broadcast commercials on the theme of football during the World Cup. The only restriction for Pepsi was to refrain from using the official symbols and titles reserved for official sponsors alone. At times, the money saved by companies that do not pay official rights—which are at times exorbitant—permits them to develop highly effective programmes by combining commercials, posters, competitions, activities, public relations, and the like to the detriment of the effectiveness of programmes on the part of official sponsors. In fact, the official sponsors must spend large amounts in order to make their sponsorship known and to communicate it.

Nike, regarding its campaign for the Football World Cup, states, "We are not carrying

---

[1] This aspect was handled in the chapter relating to brand equity management.

out ambush marketing by trying to recuperate the event. We are simply partners to teams and to players taking part in the World Cup. That makes us legitimate actors in the event. Nike has a communication programme about football, not about the World Cup". Fortunately, Adidas—which spent millions in order to be the official sponsor for the competition—was able to exploit its partnership and finally succeeded in its best media coups outside of its contracts with the French team replica shirt, winners of the 1998 World Cup and worn by many well-known personalities. The jersey was also projected as an image on the Arc de Triomphe in Paris in front of millions of spectators after the final (France on Adidas against Brazil on Nike), with the slogan "La victoire est en nous!" (Victory is in us!).

Finally, the major rival companies, impelled by the IOC, signed a charter committing them to refrain from developing ambush marketing programmes at the Sydney Olympic Games.

It is worth pointing out that this process occurs within a marketing approach for both the sponsor and the sport organisation. In the introduction of this book, we noted that the collection of funds can be marketed. The definition by Kotler, Dubois, and Manceau (2003)[2] is highly relevant in this context.

4.2 Sponsoring and Persuasive Communication

Analysis and comprehension of the mechanism of sponsoring activity are essential for achieving strategic management of sponsoring. This notably makes it possible to select opportunities, to define a strategy for action, and to evaluate the impact of this action.

Review of Literature

Cornwell and Maignan in 1998 noted that research in the area of sponsoring had not yet adopted a specific theoretical framework to guide investigations aimed at understanding the reaction of consumers to sponsoring. Analysis of the theoretical basis of research on this process of persuasive communication permits us to state that it calls on either conditioning or cognitive consistency. Here we present the most important researchers in this field.

Explanatory Models Based on the Theory of Cognitive Consistency

Crimmins and Horn (1996) analyse sponsoring as a persuasive communication process. According to these authors, "Sponsoring is a means of persuasion that is fundamentally different to traditional publicity. Sponsoring persuades indirectly". Sponsoring improves the perception of the brand by associating our beliefs and linking the brand to an event or an organisation that the audience holds in high esteem.

Crimmins and Horn (1996) analyse the persuasive effect of sponsoring as a combination of four factors.

- The strength of the link that is created between the brand and the event or organisation
- The duration of this link
- The gratitude that is felt because of this link
- The change in perception caused by this link

This mechanism of action is based on Heider's (1946) balance theory. According to this theory, each individual seeks to achieve a balanced configuration between cognitive and emotional factors. This balance is situated on the basis of three relations: the relation between the individual and the object of the attitude; the relation between the individual and a linked object (another person, a consequence); and the relation between the object of the attitude and a linked object (another individual, a consequence). There will be a balance if the three relations are positive or if two of them are negative.

According to Heider (1946), "A balanced configuration exists if attitudes to a causal unit are similar". This implies that a situation is balanced if attitudes towards two factors have the

---

[2] According to Kotler and Dubois (1992), "Marketing is the economic and social mechanism by which individuals and groups satisfy their needs and desires by means of creating and exchanging products and other entities that are of value to others".

same positive or negative orientation. If this is not the case at the outset, the related cognitive and emotional factors will tend towards a state of balance. In our opinion, this theory supports the sponsoring approach in that it concerns a "transfer of sympathy". Individuals interested in an event have a positive attitude towards it. If this is not the case for the sponsors present in the given universe, these individuals will rebalance their attitude to the sponsor in relation to their attitude to the event. A person's thought process might be, for example, "The footballer Zinedine Zidane recommends Adidas, I like Zidane a lot, and I appreciate Adidas. Michael Jordan recommends Nike, I don't like Jordan, and in turn I don't like Nike".

Explanatory Models Based on the Conditioning Process

The theory of emotional conditioning seeks to explain the emotional reactions to communication. According to this approach, a brand (conditioned stimulus) is associated with a pleasant situation (nonconditioned stimulus). Following a certain number of repetitions, the brand when presented is capable of provoking the same pleasant emotion in the individual. The experiment by Gorn (1982) is frequently cited as support for this theory. The experiment used slides to associate pleasant or unpleasant music to the presentation of a beige or a blue pen. At the end of the experiment participants received as a gift a pen of the same type, but they were allowed to choose its colour (blue or beige). The results showed that when the music was pleasant, the participants tended to choose the pen presented in the publicity; when the music was unpleasant they tended to choose the pen that was not present in the publicity. The experiment was strongly criticised, notably by Allen and Madden (1985), particularly since the results were not confirmed in other experiments reproducing the same protocol (Kellaris and Cox, 1989).

Dress (1989) applied the emotional conditioning model in the area of sponsoring. Situating his reflection at a theoretical level alone, Dress believes that emotional conditioning has a greater chance of success if the emotions associated with the products of the sponsors are close to those associated with the sport in question.

Criticisms of the Two Approaches

Despite their interest, these two approaches can be criticised. Lutz (1979) underlines two major weaknesses in Heider's theory, which concentrates only on the valency of the three relations and neglects the intensity of the relation. Moreover, the theory specifies only a single object (individual, attribute, consequence) linked to the object of the attitude. However, numerous brands have more than a single attribute and are linked to several consequences.

The concept of conditioning comes from a behaviourist perspective. It is necessary to surpass these limits. To do so, we must analyse the mechanisms of sponsoring action within a larger theoretical framework that is related to persuasive communication.

The Process Relating to Persuasive Communications

The various models of persuasive communication come from the Yale Group (Hovland, Janis, and Kelley, 1953) and in particular from the work of Hovland, Lumsdaine, and Sheffield (1945). These authors proposed analysing the persuasion mechanism based on the interaction of four factors affecting the impact of a communication: the sources, the message, the channel, and the receiver. However, the definitive version of this model was proposed in 1969. It describes a process in six phases: exposure, decoding, comprehension, acceptance, retention, and conversion into action. Beyond the rather simplistic equation (persuasion = reception × acceptance), persuasion should be viewed as including, in an indivisible manner, all six phases. Given the chain of these phases, persuasion results from the action of two processes: The first relates to reception and the second to persuasion.

Kapferer (1988), in his work on the influence of the media and of publicity on behaviour, developed an experimental model of the psychological process of persuasion. Although falling within the "Yale tradition", this author stands out regarding several points, notably the process of selective exposure to message, the allocation of attention necessary to the perception that is worked out, plus the active modification of opinions. Persuasion can be understood as "the modification of attitude and its types of behaviour by exposure to message " (Kapferer, 1988). This concept of attitude anchored in American psychology constitutes the veritable and essential causal chain.

The communication strategy based on sponsoring is likely to have an effect on a certain number of phases in this process.

1. Exposure to the message. The number of publicity messages to which a person is exposed daily is very high. We take into account only a very small number of these, either because we are not looking for information or because we wish to protect ourselves. Sponsoring is based on an event, an organisation, or an athlete who interests a certain public. This public seeks and obtains information and thus exposes itself to persuasive communications.

2. Decoding. If the sponsoring approach is well managed, notably on a level of association between the sponsor and the sponsoring support, decoding will pose no problems and the sponsor will be assimilated with the event. We deal with this process in more detail later in this section.

3. Process of acceptance or rejection. We raise the legitimacy of the link between the object of sponsoring on the one hand and the acceptance of the message conveyed by this association on the other. We have indicated that the effectiveness of sponsoring depends on the compatibility of the association (what is called the "fit") and the message communicated from this association. We have underlined that the event is a source of experiences for supporters. They experience emotions and passions, and the event stimulates their senses. This greatly favours the assimilation of the sponsor with the messages that are associated in this action.

4. Modification of the attitude. The emotional component of attitude is the most easily modified by this approach, since it is based on emotional experience. The cognitive component can also be modified. The persons involved in the event form an image of the association between the event and the sponsor. Roland Garros thus appears as a chic, elegant event, and these characteristics are likely to be transferred to a certain number of brands of sponsors of this tournament, such as Rado, Peugeot, and Perrier.

5. Stability of changes to attitude. Sponsoring has the advantage of being repetitive on condition that a long-term relation is established. Perrier has acted as the sponsor of Roland Garros for many years, but it is also the sponsor of a certain number of ATP tournaments. This permits Perrier to reactivate the link over the year while focusing on sustainability. The central question concerns the link between a change of attitude towards a sponsor and behaviour (which is expressed by a purchase or repurchase). From a theoretical point of view, this has to do with the relation between the conative component of attitude and behaviour. The model by Fishbein and Ajzen (1975) suggests that behaviour is strongly influenced by attitude and intention to purchase. This confirms the fact that, by influencing these two variables, sponsoring gives the brand an advantage over its competitors. There are, however, a large number of variables that are likely to influence purchasing behaviour, particularly in a competitive context.

Sponsoring falls perfectly within the psychological process related to persuasive communication. If well managed, the association has a powerful effect on attitude and indirectly on purchasing behaviour. The model presented, however, remains highly cognitive to the extent that the emotional component of attitude follows on from information-processing stages (comprehension of the message). We have underlined that the sport event supplies experiences and that emotion constitutes its essence. Sponsoring strategy is based on emotion. Research projects by Derbaix, Gérard, and Lardinois (1994) and Speed and Thompson (2000) have revealed, in an empirical way, the transfer of emotion between the event and the sponsor without there necessarily being activation of the cognitive processes. If the cognitive processes are indeed activated, we can presume that this takes place under the influence of the affective processes.

We shall analyse the impact of sponsoring as persuasive communication within the framework of interaction between what is cognitive and what is affective. To do so, we take the experiential framework that we presented in the second chapter. Events and the sponsoring associated with them thus supply the public with an experience based on sensations, feelings, and symbols that are likely to favour apprenticeships. According to Dussard (1983), "Apprenticeship can be defined as all the changes that affect the tendency regarding responses on the part of consumers to various stimuli and that are due to experiences".

Dynamic Model for Sponsorship

The model we present is in line with the dynamic model of the affective aspect of behaviour in consumers as proposed by Cohen and Areni (1991). The dependent variable is constituted by the three components of attitude towards the sponsor: affective (preference), cognitive (image), and behavioural (intention to purchase). The explanatory variables are the emotional reactions plus the level of cognitive handling of the information (figure 4.5).

This model is organised into three phases that are distinguished by the type of cognitive activity likely to be associated to the affective response. It should be noted that this process can be interrupted prematurely. We will see that this can influence the impact of sponsoring focused on image.

Phase 1   We show the interest of this model by taking the example of an individual who is greatly interested in the Roland Garros tennis tournament. He decides to watch the final on television because he wants to see how the tournament ends, knowing that this is the world's greatest clay court tournament, that it is part of the Grand Slam, and that it takes place in Paris. These characteristics are the most evident and belong to the heart of this tournament's identity. They constitute a promise—of a great tennis event that is a source of pleasure.

Phase 2   If this process continues, which is most frequently the case, the television viewer has an image of the association between the sponsors and the event: It is difficult for him to escape the BNP Paribas logo at the edge of the court and that of Perrier in the players' rest area. During this phase, the viewer carries out an evaluation of the pertinence of the association between Roland Garros and, for example, Perrier (this corresponds to the force of the link in the equation by Crimmins and Horn). This evaluation takes places on the basis of an emotional reaction of the type "I like it or I don't", or "legitimate or not". If the result is favourable, a transfer of the affective component of the attitude towards the

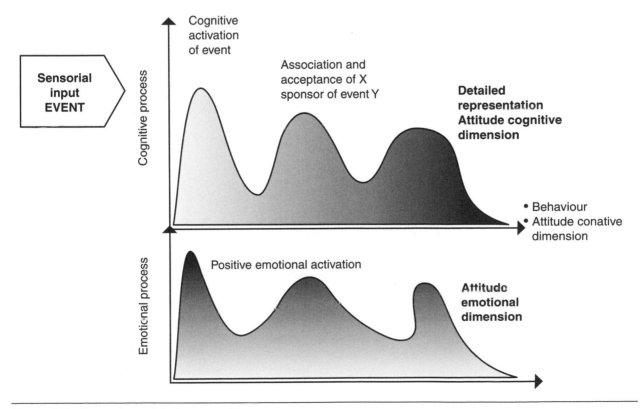

Figure 4.5   Dynamic model of sponsorship.

sponsor takes place. In fact, if the presence of the sponsor appears to be legitimate, the sponsor finds itself inserted into the affective "halo" unique to this event. In this context, a favourable attitude towards a brand does not require cognitive antecedents (expectations versus attributes). This process can be summarised as follows:

- I enjoy the Roland Garros tournament.
- Perrier is perfectly placed for this tournament.
- I enjoy Perrier.

This process is similar to that for the emotional conditioning described earlier. This has been demonstrated notably in research by Ganassali and Didellon (1996), Derbaix, Gérard, and Lardinois (1994), and Speed and Thompson (2000).

Phase 3 If the process continues further, the television viewer carries out a more detailed interpretation. This is a conscious, reflective mechanism. The image constructs that interact correspond to the concept of image or of the cognitive component of attitude. For example, the image and emotions linked to evoking the brand Perrier will interact with the image the viewer has of Roland Garros. Marion and Michel (1986) include emotional manifestations in the image. They suggest that "the image of the brand is the mental vision that the public has of a brand. This is a series of ideas, feelings, sensations, affective reactions and attitudes that are born from evoking the brand. It is the clients who create it, progressively, for themselves by using a large number of signs". Whether we make a distinction between affective and cognitive or not, it remains true that this process takes place on the basis of an affective response that is situated in extension to that of phase 2.

A television viewer generates associations with other concepts in his or her memory within a process aiming to assign supplementary meanings to them. This interaction between the two images is presented in figure 4.6.

1. Dimensions specific to the event
2. Dimensions specific to the sponsor
3. Dimensions common to the event and to the sponsor

Research carried out by Ferrand and Pagès (1996) regarding the interaction of images of the brand Perrier with the Grand Prix Tennis tournament in Lyons made it possible to identify the following dimensions:

1. Dimensions specific to the event: elegant and commercial
2. Dimension specific to Perrier: natural
3. Dimensions common to both: entertaining, dynamic, and successful

This interaction takes place on an emotional basis that combines the emotion provoked by the event with that resulting from evocation of the sponsor's brand. This repeated interaction (see discussion of duration of the link in Crimmins and Horn, 1996) is likely to reinforce existing images or generate new ones. Figure 4.7 presents the three processes resulting from this interaction:

1. Transfer of certain dimensions of the event to the sponsor
2. Reinforcement of the common dimensions between the event and the sponsor
3. Transfer of certain dimensions of the sponsor to the event

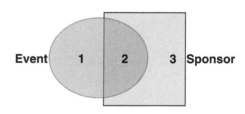

Figure 4.6 Interaction between the image of the event and the image of the sponsor (perception).

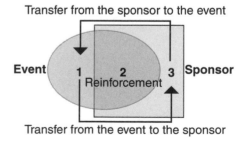

Figure 4.7 Reinforcement and transfer mechanisms on the level of interaction of the image and the event with that of the sponsor (credibility, acceptance).

The same research programme made it possible to demonstrate that this sponsoring operation reinforced the common dimensions, that is, entertaining, dynamic, and successful. The two other possibilities have yet to be validated. It is thus possible to transfer the dimension relating to elegance to the image of the brand Perrier. However, transferring the "natural" attribute to the event is theoretical because it won't add any value to this event. When a minor event associates with powerful brands such as Coca-Cola and Sony, the transfer of specific factors of the image of these brands into the event can take place (particularly if the sponsor gives its name to the event).

Work by Howard and Sheth (1969) makes it possible to explain this process. The authors recognise that alongside conditioning, a second principle of apprenticeship exists: contiguity. This principle suggests that sensations, imagery, feelings, and pleasure plus other hedonistic or symbolic components that go together within experience tend to evoke each other mutually.

To summarise, the affective responses from the first phase are immediate and automatic and are not accompanied by a real awareness process. The responses during the second phase emerge from the affective trace associated with the identified stimulus but also from the initial concept activated (the event). These responses from the second phase are still automatic and fast. If the third stage is reached, the person enters a process that leads him or her to develop a new knowledge about the event.

Activation of the Sponsor's Brand As a Catalyst

Within sponsoring focused on image, it is essential for the process to be completed. For this reason, it is necessary to activate the process by means of specific operations. What we also call valorising the action of sponsoring is a process that is increasingly well controlled. This is even imperative for sponsors of the Olympic Games who are not present at the competition venue. They must simply exploit their association with the event (figure 4.8).

There are numerous means that make it possible to activate the sponsor's brand among individuals interested in the event. We shall

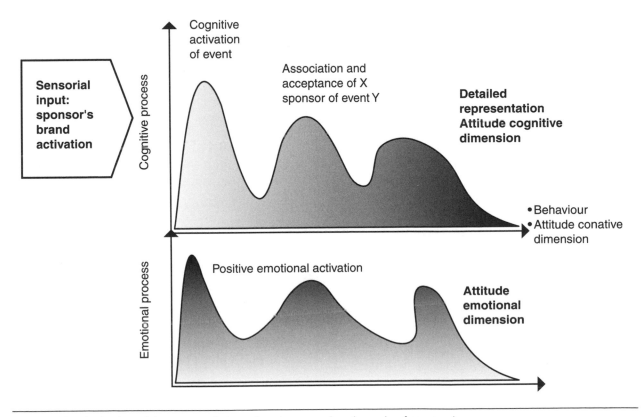

Figure 4.8 Activation of the sponsor's brand and persuasive dynamic of sponsoring.

take the example of an advertisement that refers explicitly to this sponsoring action. Perrier uses advertising in magazines that presents the terms "tennis" and "Roland Garros" in the colour (green) of the tournament and the brand, associated with yellow tennis balls. This representation of the concept leads to an emotional reaction on the basis of an attenuated reaction to the emotions felt during the tournament. The second level of reading appears with the slogan "Perrier, official bubble of Roland Garros". The objective here is to reinforce this partnership plus the feeling of gratitude. This enters into the framework of the affective response of phase 2. The more detailed development suggested by a third level of reading refers to pleasure, relaxation, and distinction. This is a question of evoking dimensions common to the two images in order to reinforce the positive attitude towards the brand.

This model also functions for team sponsoring, for sport organisations, or for athletes, as does what is called endorsement. Derbaix and Brée (2000) note that endorsement will be a success when the attributes of a star are associated with the brand in the mind of consumers. At this stage, the transfer takes the form of a translation of the significant contributions of the individual ("the star") to the brand.

It should be noted that the effects of the attitude components differ depending on the nature of the process that leads to determining them, that is, according to whether this is an emotional process or a rational one. Moreover, sponsoring can call upon rational processes on the basis of a cognitive apprenticeship. This is the case when an equipment supplier such as Prince wishes to demonstrate the performance and effectiveness of its rackets by sponsoring a player such as Patrick Rafter. It is a question of transferring functional attributes (power + precision = performance), since success in competition is considered to be credible to spectators or television viewers who play tennis.

This experiential context authorises a classical cognitive apprenticeship. In the chapter devoted to decision making by consumers, we stressed that experiential marketing views consumers as both emotional and rational. According to the cognitive conception, apprenticeship is the consequence of modification of the individual's knowledge level. The effort is to analyse the influence of the experience accumulated by the consumer over the decision-making process. The model for seeking experiences is not intended to replace the model for information processing, which remains valid on the basis of the paradigm of maximising utility. It offers an expansion of the theoretical analysis framework of persuasive communications. This framework appears well suited to the analysis of the impact of sponsoring.

4.3 Developing Strategic Choices Concerning Sponsoring

Modelling sponsoring as a persuasive communication process enables us to define the operational principles that make strategic management possible. This must be envisaged from the point of view of the sport organisation and from that of the sponsor.

In the second section of the first chapter devoted to Olympic sport organisation's brand equity, we developed a framework for measuring brand equity. This consists of three phases: market strategic analysis, conception of the brand identity system, and implementation of the brand identity. The strategy relating to sponsorship falls within this approach, which also contributes towards positioning the brand. Companies that use sponsoring, or envisage doing so, must take the following dimensions into consideration.

1. Compatibility between the image of the object that serves as a support to sponsoring and the sponsor's image

2. Acceptability and gratitude regarding the association between the sponsor and the object of sponsorship

3. Compatibility between the potential partner's strategic positioning and the possibilities offered by the interaction of the two images present

4. Compatibility between the sponsor's communication objectives and the communication possibilities

5. Coherence between the target of the event and the sponsor's communication target

6. The possibilities of activating the sponsor's brand among its communication target

7. The strength of offer from a competitive perspective

Sport organisations must develop an offer bearing all these points in mind. We illustrate this strategic analysis by examining the partnership between Elan Ski and the Slovenian Olympic Committee.

EXHIBIT 4.2 ELAN, A SLOVENE COMPANY

www.elansports.com

Elan is a Slovenian brand of sporting equipment recognised worldwide, starting with the production of skis in the early 1950s. Subsequently Elan began to supply sporting equipment for sport halls and to produce sailing boats, motor yachts, bikes, and finally clothing in the last decade. Annual production stands at more than 400,000 pairs of skis, over 80% of which are exported around the globe. The most important markets for Elan are Europe, North America, and Japan. But Elan keeps its leading role in Slovenia and in the markets of southeastern Europe (figure 4.9).

Elan's foundations are expressed in the following:

• **Tradition.** Since its foundation in 1941, Elan has contributed considerably to the development of skis and thus is justifiably proud of its close to 60 years of tradition. As the inventor of the first carved skis back in the mid-1980s, as well as many other technical innovations such as the complex core,

the parabolic sidecut, monoblock construction, the integrated plate, and the first integrated fusion binding system, Elan has a name that is now synonymous with top-quality products that provide the utmost pleasure on snow.

• **A Slovene company.** This is where Elan comes from—Slovenia, a small but successful country with a disparate and pristine environment. The Slovenes themselves are considerate but resolute. As the only ski manufacturer in Slovenia, Elan is different from its competitors. Everything takes place in Slovenia, starting with the idea and proceeding through the design concept and complex development process to the actual production. Without doubt, made in Slovenia!

• **Essence.** Following the ski market crisis of the 1990s, Elan decided to exploit a new marketing strategy. While in previous decades the company had put a lot of effort into development and cutting-edge technology, it decided instead to give its brand a new image with a new design and a different marketing approach. The aim is to create skis with excellent characteristics, with a modern, exciting—but at the same time logical—design, as well as with an optimal balance between quality and price for all categories of skier. Whoever uses an Elan ski is bound to feel the passion and the knowledge integrated into every Elan product.

• **Passion and real "tech" from Slovenia.** The company's passion is to create the best-engineered ski equipment in the world with modern designs and top performance. Nestled in the heart of the Slovenian mountains, Elan is dedicated to producing skis for people with a passion for skiing. The company sends the message to customers, "Your passion is our passion".

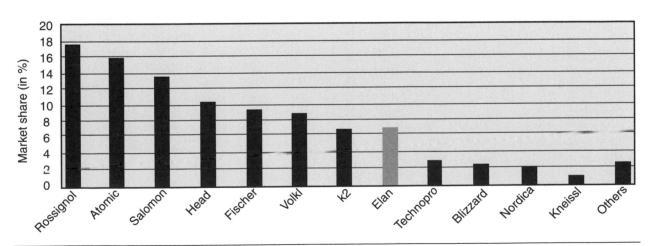

Figure 4.9 World wide ski market share.

- **Real technology.** Elan uses advanced technology throughout its collection. Its research and development department works hard to find functional materials and designs that will enhance the performance of every ski in its line.

- **100% focus.** Elan prides itself on its dedication to producing high-quality products throughout its entire collection.

Elan's Position

The Elan trademark is renowned as a Slovenian inventive brand of excellent quality, made by a company that knows how to design and manufacture equipment of the very finest quality for passionate people over the world.

- **Elan as an SOC partner.** Strategic management of Elan has been closely connected with sponsoring as a persuasive communication since the company entered the international markets in the 1970s and began using Ingemar Stenmark (Sweden), one of the best skiers of all time. Since that time the company has been using sponsoring as one of its marketing tools. Elan entered into sponsoring of the SOC immediately after the country became independent and has supported the SOC for more than 10 years.

Information and figure courtesy of Elan.

Perceived Compatibility Between SOC and Elan Brand Images

We mentioned compatibility earlier. It is time now to present an operational diagnostic method. During the first step, it is necessary to identify the attributes as well as the perceived features of the OSO brand and a sponsor's brand (figure 4.10). According to consumers' perceptions, these contents can be analysed bearing in mind four categories as presented in figure 4.10. The SOC developed the evaluation system of cooperation that at the beginning is always used as a tool to search for possible business partners. Prior to a successful start and then after a certain period of partnership (yearly base), SOC evaluates the most important attributes as well as the perceived characteristics of the SOC and Elan brands.

Functional Aspects Related to Utility Value of the Product or Service

The Elan factory produces skis, snowboards, and sporting goods of high standards and qual-

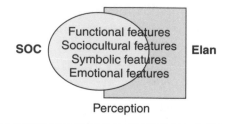

Figure 4.10 Interaction of the SOC image and that of the sponsor depending on various features.

ity at competitive prices. The company survived a difficult time in the world ski industry, selling its products to all markets and organising production for other brands. Elan is associated with innovation (carving technology and integration/fusion technology were invented by Elan) and the notion of enjoyment in performance; and with Elan marine, it became associated with technical merit and lifestyle.

The SOC is a relatively new organisation concentrating on top performance of athletes, good organisation, and Sport for All activities. It benefits from the Olympic Games, the largest sporting event. According to the global marketing research conducted by Meridian, the Olympic Games embodies the following attributes in the minds of people worldwide: multicultural, global, friendship, participation, fair competition, determination, honourable, peaceful, patriotic, festive.

Sociocultural Factors

An OSO or company brand is the product of a culture. The associated benefits convey an added value of a social and cultural nature: a social link, a lifestyle, social status, values.

- Elan: sense of accomplishment, an exciting life, freedom, ambitious, capable, courageous, imaginative, responsible
- Slovenian National Olympic Committee: sense of accomplishment, a world at peace, an exciting life, freedom, ambitious, capable, courageous, imaginative, responsible, true friendship

The Elan brand is associated with Slovenian culture, identity, and the importance of sport as a part of the everyday life of a Slovenian family. The association between the Elan brand and SOC gives added value to both partners with their social, cultural, or business activities. As

Elan supports top athletes through SOC and some NFs, it supports a wide variety of sports and also supports handicapped athletes. One of the activities with a strong social link is an event called "Top Athletics for Handicapped Athletes", an all-day sporting culture event held at the company. Organised with the support of the SOC, it is a gathering of athletes, coaches, and staff in addition to people from the business environment and local authorities. Elan demonstrates its core values as a socially responsible company.

Symbolic and Imaginary Factors

The most visible factors are the symbols of each brand (figure 4.11). The Elan logo changed once during its history and has evolved into two forms: the company name, written in green, and a green letter *e*. The SOC logo consists of Slovenian symbols—the sea and the highest Slovenian mountain (Mt. Triglav)—and includes the Olympic rings. Both brands are well recognised, and the logos are used to form a composite logo for Elan's communication with its target groups.

SLOVENIA

SPONSOR OF THE SLOVENIAN OLYMPIC TEAM

Figure 4.11 Sponsee and sponsor composite logo.
Courtesy of the Slovenian Olympic Committee.

Emotional Factors

In the second chapter we stressed that sport provides an emotional experience (figure 4.12). The SOC represents the most important sporting organisation in the country, with top athletes winning at the Olympic Games, and Slovenians identify themselves through this. Supporting the Slovenian Olympic team provokes various positive emotions such as pleasure, contentment, peacefulness, and optimism and sometimes some emotions that are negative such as sadness. Elan as a company that wins in business and as the supplier of excellent sporting goods provides emotions such as pleasure, contentment, pride, enjoyment, and satisfaction.

After performing a content analysis of the SOC and Elan images separately, it is important to determine if they have some specific or common characteristics. A simple table that presents the four categories of benefits (functional, sociocultural, symbolic, and emotional) in relation to their status (specific to sponsee, specific to sponsor, and common to sponsee and sponsor) is a useful tool to make this determination. This diagnostic is carried out on a level of what is perceived, that is, on an image level. The major characteristics concerning SOC and Elan are shown in table 4.1.

Acceptability of the Association

Speed and Thompson (2000) conceived a tool that makes it possible to analyse a certain number of dimensions resulting from the interaction between the object of sponsorship and

Figure 4.12 Emotion is a part of the game.
Courtesy of the Slovenian Olympic Committee.

the sponsor. Among these, we retain two that are particularly useful for the diagnostic. These are the strength of the link between the event and the sponsor, and the perceived sincerity of the sponsor's action.

Strength of the Link Between Sponsor and Sport Organisation

The strength of the link between the sponsor and the event is assessed based on four proposals. Individuals questioned are invited to respond using a six-step scale[3]:

1. There is a logical connection between the SOC and Elan.
2. Elan and the SOC go well together.
3. Elan and the SOC wish to express the same things.
4. For me, it's logical for Elan to sponsor the SOC.

Perceived Sincerity of Sponsor and Gratitude Towards the Sponsor

The perceived sincerity of the sponsor must be assessed after an event. It is appreciated based on two proposals that individuals respond to on a six-step scale from "fully agree" to "fully disagree".

1. Sport basically benefits from this sponsoring.
2. The main reason that leads the sponsor to become involved is that it believes that the SOC deserves support.

Gratitude towards the sponsor can be assessed based on the proposal (six-step scale from "fully agree" to "fully disagree") "We can say thank you for Elan's support".

Compatibility Between Strategic Positioning of the Partner's Brand and the Possibilities From Interaction

We must recall that image is an emission concept that refers to a perceived reality. Identity, for its part, is an emission concept. Sponsoring has a direct relation with the communication of an identity. For the sport organisation, this

Table 4.1 Interaction Between SOC and Elan Brand Image Characteristics

	Specific to SOC	Common to SOC and Elan	Specific to Elan
Functional characteristics	All sports Top sport event Top sport results Sport for All	Know-how Top for All Quality Well managed	Ski and snowboard Innovation Enjoyment with top sport and recreational products
Sociocultural characteristics	National True friendship Courageousness Fair play Respect	Slovenian Tradition Sense of accomplishment An exciting life Ambition Responsible Capable	Ambitious Serious Imaginative
Symbolic characteristics	Logo with national symbols and Olympic rings		Elan logo in green or letter *e* as a fresh brand
Emotional characteristics	Passion Optimism Happiness Peacefulness	Pride Pleasure Contentment	Enjoyment Satisfaction

---

[3] 6. Fully agree; 5. Agree; 4. Partly agree; 3. Partly disagree; 2. Disagree; 1. Fully disagree.

diagnostic is fairly difficult to carry out, because only the strategic core that manages the brand fully masters the subject. It is nevertheless possible to acquire information by analysing the content of the communication regarding the brand and by analysing the possibilities following the image diagnostic.

Given the diagnostic on the level of compatibility between the two images, there are two possibilities on a strategic level:

- Reinforcing in people's minds the common characteristics (central column in the table 4.1)
- Transferring some specific event-related characteristics to the sponsor's image (figure 4.13)

The first strategy is nearly risk free because it is already perceived by the communication target. The second strategy implies to change people's perception of the sponsor's brand. However, the credibility of this strategy must be tested.

The question is one of defining a strategy relating to the emission by responding to the following questions:

- What message should be communicated to the target?
- Will this message be judged credible by the target?
- Will it have the expected effect on attitude towards the brand?

To do this, it is necessary to evaluate the interaction between the two entities more precisely, taking into account dimensions that can be actively communicated to the target and legitimated by sponsoring. These are of three types:

1. "Natural" links group together dimensions that are both accepted by the target and relevant from a marketing perspective. "Common" links are part of this category. Certain more distant dimensions that are specific can be accepted by individuals involved with the event. For this reason, it is worthwhile "testing" these distant associations in order to verify their acceptance by the individuals targeted.

2. The "dilemma" links concern dimensions that are not fully accepted by the target, or are not relevant from a strategic perspective, or both. However, this situation is likely to evolve over time because of valorisation actions.

3. The "don't go" links unite the dimensions that are not accepted by the target or are not relevant strategically.

Each dimension can therefore be taken into the matrix of perceived distance versus credibility of the link presented in figure 4.14.

Elan as a sport brand actively communicates the following position: tradition, passion, invention, and real technology from Slovenia. We can construct the matrix presented in figure 4.15.

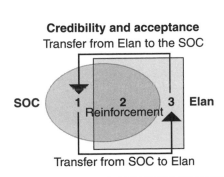

Credibility and acceptance
Transfer from Elan to the SOC

Figure 4.13 Analysis of the acceptability of strategic choices.

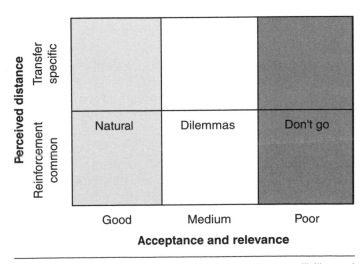

Figure 4.14 Matrix of perceived distance versus credibility and relevance of the link.

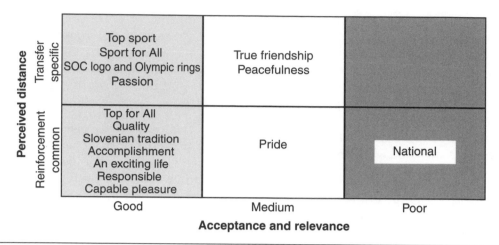

Figure 4.15 Matrix of perceived distance versus credibility and relevance of the link for the SOC and Elan.

The short version of this matrix situates the natural links on a level of common characteristics such as Top Sport, Sport for All, fair play, SOC logo associated with the Olympic rings, passion, Top for All, quality, Slovenian, tradition, accomplishment, an exciting life, responsible, capable, pleasure. The dilemmas refer to true friendship and peacefulness, which are not fully accepted, and pride, which is not relevant in a strategic perspective. National belongs to the "don't go" category because of Elan's international strategy.

Compatibility Between Sponsor's Communication Objectives and the Possibilities

Elan as producer of sporting equipment communicates with national and international markets, about top-quality products not only for top sport results, but more importantly for pleasure, enjoyment, and innovation for people who engage in sport as one of the basic human needs. Elan sponsors the SOC, its selected member federations, and clubs and athletes from the top to the junior level. Elan reaches all sporting target groups through sponsoring the SOC. Through involvement in the Sport for All events the company is able to create links with people who do sports for fun, pleasure, and health; and Elan reinforces its positioning and fits with the perceived image of SOC. Why an international focus? Elan intends to put Slovenia on the world map; that is, this company wants to increase its awareness among Olympic sport fans.

Sport for All events organised under the umbrella of SOC consist of running, cycling, mountaineering, skiing, and other all-year events. Through these it is possible for Elan to bring in experiences that are well suited to consumption of its various products. Above all these events reinforce the affective and cognitive association between experience among different target groups and a healthy, convivial environment, as well as developing the Elan reflex according to the brand's strategic positioning.

Coherence Between the Organisation's and Sponsor's Communication Targets

Elan looks for both national and international communication targets. Slovenian athletes participate in the largest sport events. According to a Meridian analysis, broadcasts of the Sydney Olympic Games ultimately reached 3.7 billion viewers in a record 220 countries. Nine out every 10 individuals on the planet with access to television watched some part of the Olympics. An average of 19 hours of airtime every day were dedicated to coverage of the Sydney 2000 Olympic Games. Furthermore the Olympic Games are unique among sporting events because they attract similar audiences of male (55%) and female (45%) viewers.

In Slovenia, keen television viewing interest in the Olympic Games was expressed by 46% of the population, and 47% had a casual interest. Furthermore, research on Slovenian sporting activities undertaken by the Institute of Sport from Ljubljana shows that approximately 40% of the population is actively engaged in sport; 15% of all Slovenes are members of various sporting organisations; and 13% of children are active in school sport clubs. The SOC counts 59 sport associations and 89 regional organisations; these cover the majority of organised sports in the country. Member associations have over 3,000 clubs and over 300,000 members.

Consequently, the fit between the international and the Slovenian Olympic movement audiences and Elan's communication and marketing target is fairly good.

Possibilities of Sponsor's Activating Its Brand Among the Communication Target

The activation process depends on the needs of both business partners, resulting in the analysis of needs prior to the start of cooperation, always at the beginning of the relationship, and then on a yearly basis. Elan uses different departments of the SOC and its activities to communicate to target groups regarding its products. In general, top sport results, events, and athletes serve to promote and activate products that are presented at Sport for All events and marketed in the Elan sport shop network.

In this context, activation is based on the three following dimensions:

1. Status position of sponsor
2. Exposure of the sponsor in the media, which includes independent discounts
3. Direct access to key sporting partners (national and international), business environment, and target public

Status Position

For the sponsor, status position includes the following benefits: identification with a unique nonpolitical worldwide sports organisation; use of SOC logotype and its trademark; identification with an image of the best athletes-winners; and exposure to fans and to public. These benefits are outlined in the following sections.

Identification With a Unique Nonpolitical Worldwide Sport Organisation The Olympic rings are the most recognisable logotype in the world according to research results. No one except the SOC partners and Top partners has the right to identify with the SOC. Olympic team sponsors have exclusive advantages and a special position in society. The SOC protects them and the International Olympic Committee Top partners against ambush in the country. This is shown in international and Slovenian research (Mediana, 2001, 2002, 2003).

Use of SOC Logotype and Its Trademark The IOC works to protect the value inherent in the Olympic rings as the most recognised icon in the world and encourages the rest of the Olympic family to do so. This legislation culminates in the Olympic Arrangement Act.

The trademark and its use are in the complete ownership of the SOC and are not transferable. The trademark and SOC logotype can be used in accordance with SOC graphic manual, which includes complete SOC graphic images.

Sponsors can use the logotype and the "Olympic team sponsor" trademark in all forms of marketing and public relations for products and services as agreed to in contracts. With the SOC trademark, they can present themselves in public, which is true for all visual trademarks of this status on various promotional and other material.

Identification With Image of the Best Athletes and Winners Athletes are an excellent promotional platform for the country, and their images are becoming a part of successful Slovenian marketing communications. Research shows that Slovenes prefer companies that invest in sport and that use athletes' images to promote their products. The image of the athlete is thereby transferred to the image of the company and its products (figure 4.16, *a* and *b*).

Exposure to Fans and Public Sponsors are entitled to publicly use the SOC trademark, which is true also for other visual trademarks of this kind on various promotional and other material and events.

The SOC has built its media net, and regularly prepares PR materials and advertisements, using different communication tools. Before and after events (Top Sport and Sport for All) are organised, various materials are produced by media (electronic and printed) or by SOC itself. Printed matter and other SOC

Figure 4.16 *(a)* Elan's sport equipment catalogue showing bronze medal-winning athletes from the Salt Lake City Winter Olympics. *(b)* Elan's catalogue showing silver medal winners in volleyball EYOF 2003, Paris, wearing Elan clothing.
Courtesy of the Slovenian Olympic Committee.

promotional material are issued systematically. The SOC is producing an SOC bulletin, *Olympic News,* in printed and electronic form (figure 4.17); informative Olympic team presentation pamphlets; Olympic poster table calendars; and other materials.

The Elan logo is systematically exposed, and Elan has the right to use these materials for advertising and promotion. At the same time Elan has the right to present its own Olympic- and sport-related activities in materials (figure 4.18).

Sponsor Exposure in Media Including Independent Discounts

The SOC cooperates with several media, considering the reputation surrounding its activities as well as its sponsors and other business partners. For this purpose, it operates in conjunction with national media—electronic (RTV Slovenija) and printed *(Dnevnik, Večer)*—and a network of local and regional TV and radio stations that take care of Olympic team sponsor recognition in all Slovenian regions. The SOC concludes special arrangements that guarantee lower prices with all cooperating media for its

Figure 4.17 *Olympic News* edited by the SOC.
Courtesy of the Slovenian Olympic Committee.

Figure 4.18 An SOC presentation panel with Elan's logo included.
Courtesy of the Slovenian Olympic Committee.

business partners. Regular emissions on electronic media and in the newspapers provide sponsors additional extra commercial appearances and public relations.

A sponsor is entitled to introduce itself at the official presentation of the Olympic team, which takes place before the Olympic Games, and at the presentation of the Olympic athletes and equipment in national, regional, and local media (figure 4.19, a and b). Elan, as with other

sponsors, has the rights for presentation at Sport for All events around the county and other SOC events and press conferences.

Direct Access to Key Sporting Partners, Business Environment, and Targeted Audience

SOC sponsors are also getting these opportunities: cooperation with SOC connected institutions, indirect business contacts in the Olympic family include a visit by the sponsor's representative to the Olympic Games, cooperation with SOC business partners, direct collaboration with Slovenian athletes, sport associations and clubs.

Cooperation With SOC-Connected Institutions The SOC as a sport organisation unites 89 municipal sport associations and national branches of sport associations as well as the most successful Slovenian companies. It closely cooperates with the IOC and its marketing agency, Meridian, whereby it supports sponsors' projects with financial funds. Elan has implemented leisure-time clothing, a new brand called the Slovenian Olympic Collection (figure 4.20).

Visits of Sponsor's Representative to Olympic Games Each sponsor has the right to visit the Olympic Games (Summer and Winter) twice during each Olympic cycle and can invite its business partners (figure 4.21). This gives the sponsor the right to indirect establishment of business contacts in the Olympic family. Within the framework of the visiting programme that

a

b

Figure 4.19 *(a)* Slovenian Olympic athletes' reception organized by the Mercator department store, an SOC sponsor. *(b)* Athletes have used the Elan Olympic collection, which was the best promotion for clothing after success and medals.

(a) Courtesy of the Slovenian Olympic Committee. *(b)* Courtesy of Elan.

Figure 4.20 Young athletes with first test edition of national track suit.

Courtesy of the Slovenian Olympic Committee.

Figure 4.21 VIP Elan house, where the SOC organised several receptions and press conferences.

Courtesy of the Slovenian Olympic Committee.

Figure 4.22 The Slovenian Salt Lake City Winter Olympic team at SKB bank, an SOC sponsor, wearing the Elan Olympic collection. The campaign of SOC, SKB bank, and Visa (IOC sponsor) for the Visa card benefited Elan clothing.

Courtesy of SKB Bank.

the SOC prepares for its sponsors, the sponsors receive special treatment as VIP guests, enabling them to make business contacts with other companies (domestic and foreign sponsors' representatives) and assist them in establishing own their VIP facilities and promotional programmes.

Cooperation With SOC Business Partners For sponsors of the SOC there are regular meetings (sponsors' clubs, marketing committee, sport marketing-related seminars) in which strategy, appearances, and other related matters are discussed and the SOC encourages sponsors to prepare common products related to Olympic matters. For example, Elan as official Olympic team equipment sponsor, in cooperation with the SOC as partner and a company named Rokus, started an "Olympic challenge" campaign for children from 9 to 15 in which all Slovenian schoolchildren were invited to be a part of the game. During their visit to EYOF Paris, the sponsors met marketing representatives of the French Olympic Committee and exchanged experiences regarding the cooperation of the business community in sport projects. The very successful French Winter Olympic Games campaign was presented, and Elan decided it would give even stronger support to the Torino 2006 Olympic Games (figure 4.22).

Direct Collaboration Opportunities With Slovenian Athletes, Sport Associations, and Clubs Product and service promotion with the best athletes leads to a company's recognition and enhanced reputation (figure 4.23). The SOC assists sponsors in establishing contacts with individual sport associations, clubs, and athletes. Sponsors have the right to cooperate with Olympic athletes for the purpose of their marketing needs with respect to IOC rules.

Competitiveness of Offers in a Competitive Perspective

Offer competitiveness depends on the sponsor's return on investment in a competitive context. Olympic sport organisations can be in two situations according to whether it is a question of renewing a sponsor's contract or recruiting a new partner. In both cases it is necessary to set up a service allowing evaluation of the results in connection with current or potential sponsor expectations.

123

Figure 4.23 After the Salt Lake City Olympic Games, Elan launched its own campaign for a clothing collection.

Courtesy of Elan.

A return on investment (ROI) procedure was developed and upgraded both by Elan and SOC in collaboration with partner companies specialising in communication impact assessment and market research. This procedure is presented in figure 4.24 with regard to measuring so-called soft and hard benefits for sponsors.

Elan's ROI is related to the SOC sponsorship programme and its activation programmes; Elan's strategy aims to develop links with an activation strategy by the brand, around sponsoring. Sponsoring is combined with promotions, new product placements and tests of the sporting equipment, traditional publicity, and PR and advertising in the SOC media net. At the same time Elan uses offered events and activities of the SOC as product distribution channels. The presence of Elan at competitive sponsored events, but also the creation of specific events for the target public to reactivate the messages, and finally endorsement strategies at Sport for All events providing role models, gives credibility to both partners.

Elan gets more publicity by using SOC media channels for advertising, PR, and appearances in sporting programmes and newspapers and other media (figure 4.25). The company is upgrading the sales promotion and sales process in general in its own sporting goods shops using top athletes and presenting Slove-

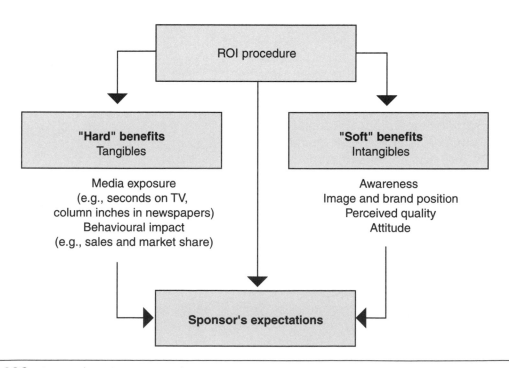

Figure 4.24 The SOC return on investment procedure.

nian Olympic Collection sport clothing. Both exposure of Elan and behaviour of target groups are easy to measure and in the short term more influential on cooperation and the sponsoring process, but "soft benefits" such as recognition, cognition, brand awareness, brand position, and brand image are crucial for the long-term prosperity of the company.

The strength of the link between Elan (and all SOC sponsors) and the SOC is assessed yearly through the research of partner company Mediana on a representative sample of the country and with other research-targeted management of the sponsor company. When researching public opinion it is essential to get information about the perception related

Figure 4.25 The SOC providing, with the assistance of a partner company, a special service for measuring media appearances to Elan.

Courtesy of the Slovenian Olympic Committee.

to sponsoring, sponsor companies' positions, and their relation to the SOC. It is interesting that Elan is investing less in direct advertising than are other branches who are sponsors of SOC but has better recognition among the researched population. Table 4.2 shows results regarding five attributes for three selected companies that are sponsors of the SOC.

4.4 Conclusion

This chapter enabled us to specify the persuasive impact of sponsoring in order to develop a model that makes it possible to work out strategic choices relating to sponsorship. This is presented in figure 4.26. It can be used both by OSO marketers and sponsors. This model is structured in five sections.

A. Diagnosis of the Central Core Relating to Compatibility of Association ("FIT")

This aspect was largely illustrated in the previous sections. It is a question of carrying out a diagnosis relating to the compatibility of association between an OSO and sponsor brands. We are in the core of the process. If this diagnosis demonstrates that the criteria in their entirety are not satisfied, it will be appropriate to give up the process.

Table 4.2 **SOC Sponsor Ratings**

	Sponsor recognition	Company performance	Brand to consider	Brand goodwill	Use of products or services
Elan	4.60	4.50	4.51	4.53	2.75
SKB	5.00	4.88	4.43	4.40	2.76
Pivovarna Laško	5.00	4.70	5.00	5.00	4.40

Scale from 1 (low) to 5 (high).

Data from the Slovenia Olympic Committee.

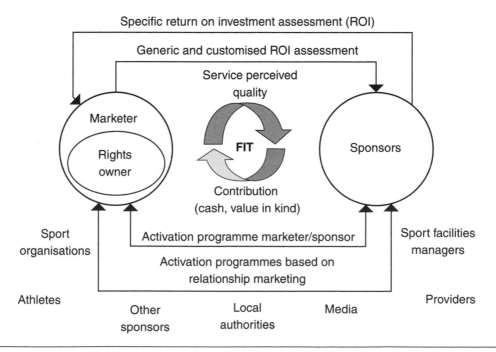

Figure 4.26 Strategic sponsorship model.

1. Compatibility between the image of the object that serves as a support to sponsoring and the sponsor's image
2. Acceptability and gratitude relating to the association between the sponsor and the object of sponsorship
3. Compatibility between the potential partner's strategic positioning and the possibilities offered by the interaction of the two images
4. Compatibility between the sponsor's communication objectives and the communication possibilities
5. Coherence between the target of the event and the sponsor's communication target
6. Conceded rights, exploitation and ambush protection

B. Evaluation of the Perceived Quality of the Basic Sponsoring Programme

1. Structure of the sponsorship programme, other sponsors involved, data, customised fit analysis
2. OSO stakeholders
3. Programme perceived quality: tangible aspects, empathy, responsiveness, reassurance

C. Activation Programme's Perceived Quality

1. OSO/Sponsor bilateral programme's perceived quality
2. Opportunities and existing activation programmes based on relationship marketing with OSO stakeholders and providers

D. Return on Investment Assessment

1. Existing ROI programme run by OSO
2. Relevance and cost of a specific ROI programme run by the sponsor

E. Contribution in Cash or in Value in Kind

1. Contribution amount (cash or value in kind)
2. Payment agreements and guarantees (risk)
3. Offer competitiveness

For the sport organisation, the challenge is now to develop a coherent and systematic sales policy that will guarantee the success of its sponsoring programmes.

Conclusion

Within the framework of this book, we develop four major strategic issues for OSO marketing in order to help you

- develop a deeper understanding of the principles and application of brand equity management and its importance to OSO brand building,
- analyse and understand prospective and existing stakeholders' expectations and needs and the decision-making process in order to create the right experience,
- define a marketing strategy and the internal and external influences affecting it, and
- manage the sponsorship system both to create sponsorship opportunities and to satisfy your sponsors.

We have presented concepts and methods relevant for OSO managers and have illustrated them with cases taken from practice. In this conclusion our intention is to stress the importance of human resources in the context of strategic and operational marketing.

1. Olympic Sport Organisations Are Getting Into Marketing

Any OSO defines its statutory mission by the very fact of becoming a reality. Its overriding goal is to achieve its statutory objectives. In order to do so, it must create and manage its tangible and intangible resources in the best possible way. A "marketing spirit" will permit it to define the following: the target groups, the services and products it can develop to satisfy these groups, and plans aimed at implementing strategies corresponding to its mission of mutually satisfactory exchanges—and all this while maximising its resources.

An OSO falls within a competitive framework where it will have a place among other sport organisations competing with each other as well as among commercial entities proposing rival or alternative products and services in various leisure areas. The sport organisation also forms part of an overall political, sociodemographic, economic, and technological framework that evolves over time and space. A marketing approach is thus necessary in order to promote the organisation's mission in a differentiated way among its target groups.

Generally speaking, the objectives of marketing in sport organisations are to promote their mission, to improve the awareness of their sport among selected target groups, to stimulate the population to practise every facet of their sport, to communicate an image that is coherent with the positioning of their products and services, to increase the diffusion of their sport in the media, and, finally, to secure sufficient financial resources.

Sport executives act as the vehicle of these marketing tactics within the organisation. Usually, the task of formalising and developing these objectives falls upon the marketing director, the board, or the president. More precisely, this person must identify the target groups of the sport organisation and choose among the offers to which he or she can respond in a satisfactory and competitive way. For this person, it is thus a question of implementing the strategies, plans, structure, and means that will enable target groups to know the values of the organisation's products and services and will enable the organisation to distribute these among the public in order for them to be consumed. From an operational point of view, the marketing department must develop programmes that will permit this exchange to take place in a sustainable way.

This book is not, however, intended for marketing managers alone, but for all executives in sport organisations: Marketing tactics concern everyone. We aim to help readers improve their efficiency and effectiveness by developing their competencies in sport marketing in order to better manage the sport organisation.

2. Human Resources Can Be the Best Asset or a Major Weakness for an OSO

Strategic marketing requires specific competences related to human resources. The implementation of this method will lead you to invest in your collaborators to develop their competences. It is important to stress that staff is the most significant OSO component that operates in the field of the services. A specific characteristic of OSOs is that their staffs are composed of professionals and volunteers. As a manager you have to tackle some important issues:

- Involvement: The task of achieving staff involvement is crucial for the implementation of a marketing strategy.
- Culture and aims: You must ensure that the culture and the aims of the staff fit with your strategy.
- Collaboration: You must ensure the interactions of OSO departments and must ensure that organisational staff work together towards the strategy.

Investing in people and their capacities to work as a team is the basis of the construction of a sustainable and durable competitive advantage.

3. Resistance to Change

People often resist change even if those affected will get some tangible benefits. There are a number of reasons why a given individual might feel resistant to a particular change, but several major reasons stand out. The first has to do with self-interest. When people hear about a change, they have a natural tendency to ask, "How will this change affect me?" and "Is it going to be positive for me?" The level of resistance is directly related to how strongly the individual feels his or her self-interests are affected. Sometimes things that might appear to be minor issues to one individual or group will seriously affect another person. Furthermore, changes may be good for one part of an organisation but somewhat detrimental to another part. Other common reasons for resisting change are misunderstanding and lack of trust. People frequently resist change when they misunderstand the nature of the change. Resistance increases when cultural gaps and a low level of trust between managers and staff are present. Finally, individuals differ in their ability to adjust to change, with some having a low tolerance for change. As a result, they sometimes resist change because they fear that they will not be able to learn the new skills and behaviours necessitated by the change.

Part of a manager's job is to diagnose the potential reasons why individuals who must be involved in a change might resist it. This assessment helps managers choose a means of overcoming resistance. Otherwise, their efforts to foster innovation and change may be unexpectedly broadsided. In addition, you may think that your collaborators resist a change because they are anchored in their practices. However, to implement your marketing process, you will have to change the culture of the company while acting on human resources.

Internal marketing helps to overcome resistance to change. It informs and involves all staff in new initiatives and strategies. It obeys the same rules as external marketing and has a similar structure. The main difference is that your customers are staff and colleagues from your own organisation.

4. Getting Into the "Marketing Spirit" Using Experiential Learning

Our stated objective is to permit you to promote the "marketing spirit" in your organisation and to develop winning marketing strategies, whether you are a marketing director or an active executive in a wider sense within your organisation.

Another important element is our psychological profile as a manager. Our ways of grasping situations are all different, and we analyse problems in different ways when we are under stress and must find solutions rapidly. We often think that marketing management is useful, but on some occasions we think we have no time to develop all the stages of the approach: We need to find the financing and the partners. If we fail with the strategy of our organisation, we will also fail in marketing. However, it is precisely here that the right choices must be made and that we should concentrate on the most important segments of our organisation. Of course, it is first essential to know what these are!

At times the diversity of executives' psychological profiles means that making decisions and defining the right priorities in a sport organisation are not easy tasks. According to Ferguson (1981), there are "rational" managers who wish to carry out in-depth analysis before stating their decision; others, more "doer" types, above all wish to take action and not waste time. All can be analysed via the four major types found in our psychological profiles and are linked to our right or left brain attributes.

• The "thinker" derives satisfaction by taking a problem and finding the solution to it via faultless organisation within which every alternative is examined closely. This person is meticulous, precise, and rational, but also practical and independent. However, he or she at times can be talkative, hesitant, cold, somewhat inflexible, and insensitive.

• The "feeler" above all favours social contact. This person prefers to solve human problems above all else. He or she can be empathetic and warm but also can sometimes be jealous and sentimental. The "feeler" often opposes the "thinker" in his or her approach.

• The "intuitor" is a creative person who enjoys taking part in developing the plan but not in being in charge of its operation. This person is not always realistic and stable, but often has good ideas and is oriented towards the future.

• Finally, the "sensor" focuses on results, responsibilities, and authority. This person is practical and does not lack self-confidence. He or she can be impatient and arrogant, and is anchored in the present.

Our profiles are all a combination of these dimensions, and vary depending on the situation.

A "marketing spirit" means taking a sound marketing approach, whatever the profile of the executives involved, by adapting the degree of detail in the various stages according to the context and depending on the resources available. After all, we are all pursuing the same objective: that of assuring the mission of our sport organisation and the accomplishment of our own fundamental needs.

This book is the product of an individual and collective experience within the MEMOS network. We conceived it as a reference that you will be able to confront with your practice in order to progress in the control of complexity. This confrontation will bring you into a specific learning process: the experiential learning. This type of learning occurs when managers reflect upon the activity, use their analytical skills to derive some useful insight from the experience, and then incorporate their new understanding(s) into their daily lives.

"We don't receive wisdom; we must discover it for ourselves after a journey that no one can take for us or spare us". (Marcel Proust)

Acronyms

AGFIS	General Association of International Sports Federations
AMA	American Marketing Association
ANOC	Association of National Olympic Committees
ATP	Association of Tennis Professionals
EYOF	European Youth Olympic Festival
CES	Consumption Emotion Set
EC	European Community
ECTM	European Community Trade Mark
ENGSO	European nongovernmental sport organisation
EOC	European Olympic Committee
FIBA	Fédération Internationale de Basketball
FIDAL	Federazione Italiana di Atletica Leggera
FIFA	Fédération Internationale de Football Association
FIVB	Fédération Internationale de Volley Ball
FLKERS	foundation, legal protection, knowledge, experience, relationship, stakeholders
ICAS	International Council of Arbitration for Sport
IPA	importance performance analysis
IMC	integrated marketing communication
KSF	key success factor
NOC	National Olympic Committee
IFs	International Federations
IOC	International Olympic Committee
NF	National Federation
NOCs	National Olympic Committees
NPO	non-profit organisation
OCOG	Organising Committee Olympic Games
OHIM	Office for Harmonization in the Internal Market
OL	Olympique Lyonnais
OMPI	World Organisation of Intellectual Property
OSO	Olympic sport organisation
SDCA	Sustainable and Defensible Competitive Advantage
SOC	Slovenian Olympic Committee
SPCS	Société de Participation dans les Clubs Sportifs
UCI	Union Cycliste Internationale
UEFA	Union of European Football Associations
WADA	World Anti-Doping Agency
WHO	World Health Organization

References

Aaker, D.A. 1991. *Managing brand equity: Capitalizing on the value of a brand name.* New York: Free Press.

Aaker, D.A. 1996. *Building strong brands.* New York: Free Press.

Aaker, D.A. 2001. *Strategic market management* (6th ed.). Hoboken, NJ: Wiley.

Aaker, D.A., and K.L. Keller. 1990. Consumer evaluations of brand extensions. *Journal of Marketing* 54(1), 27-41.

Abimbola, T., J. Saunders, and A.J. Broderick. 1999. Brand intangible assets evaluation: A conceptual framework. *Proceedings of the Chartered Institute of Marketing Research Seminar. Assessing marketing performance,* Cookham, 1-18.

Allen, C.T., and T.J. Madden. 1985. A closer look at classical conditioning. *Journal of Consumer Research* 12, 301-315.

Andreasen, A.R. 1965. Attitudes and consumer behaviour: A decision model. In *New research in marketing,* ed. L.E. Preston. Berkeley, CA: Institute of Business and Economics Research, University of California.

Andreasen, A.R. 1995. *Marketing social change.* San Francisco: Jossey-Bass.

Ansoff, H.I. 1965. *Corporate strategy.* New York: McGraw-Hill.

Assael, H. 1998. *Consumer behaviour and marketing action.* Cincinnati: South-Western College.

Barthes, R. 1957. *Mythologies.* Paris: Seuil.

Baumann, M. 2000. *Les 199 check-lists du marketing.* Paris: Editions d'Organisation.

Bazzanella, P. 2003. Developing sport event brand equity: The Marcialonga case. MEMOS diss. Université Claude Bernard, Lyon.

Beccarini, C. 2001. Les antécédents de la satisfaction des supporters abonnés. PhD diss., Université Claude Bernard, Lyon.

Bourdieu, P. 1979. *La distinction, critique sociale du jugement.* Paris: Editions de Minuit.

Bourgeois, L.J. 1980. Strategy and the environment: A conceptual integration. *Academy of Management Review* 5, 25-39.

Bréchignac-Roubaud, B. 2000. *Le marketing des services: Du projet au plan marketing.* Paris: Editions d'Organisation.

Brochand, B., and J. Lendrevie. 2000. *Le nouveau publicitor.* Paris: Dalloz.

Bromberger, C. 1995. *Le match de football.* Paris: Editions de la Maison des Sciences de l'Homme.

Bromberger, C. 1997. Football: La passion partisane. *Sciences Humaines,* hors série, 15, 23-26.

Bromberger, C. 1999. *La partita di Calcio: Etnologia di una passione.* Rome: Editori Riuniti.

Bromberger, C., A. Hayot, and J.M. Mariottini. 1987. Aller l'OM! Forza Juve! La passion pour le football à Marseille et à Turin, Terrain. *Carnet du Patrimoine Ethnologique* 8.

Brown, G. 1952. Brand loyalty: Fact or fiction. *Advertising Age* 23(1), 52-55.

Brustad, R.J. 1992. Integrating socialization influences into the study of children's motivation in sport. *Journal of Sport and Exercise Psychology* 14, 59-77.

Chappelet, J.L. 2004. Strategic management of Olympic sport organisations. In *Strategic and performance management of Olympic sport organisations,* ed. J.L. Chappelet and E. Bayle. Champaign, IL: Human Kinetics.

Chappelet, J.L., and E. Bayle. 2004. *Strategic and performance management of Olympic sport organisations.* Champaign, IL: Human Kinetics.

Cohen, J.B., and C.S. Areni. 1991. Affect and consumer behaviour. In *Handbook of consumer behavior,* ed. T.S. Robertson and H.H. Kassarjian. Englewood Cliffs, NJ: Prentice Hall.

Cooper, A., and P. Simons. 1997. Brand equity life stage: An entrepreneurial revolution. TBWA Simons Palmer, September.

Cornwell, B.T., and I. Maignan. 1998. An international review of sponsorship research. *Journal of Advertising* 27(1), 1-21.

Cova, B., and M. Roncaglio. 1999. Repérer et soutenir des tribus de consommateurs? *Décision Marketing* 16, 43-50.

Crimmins, J., and M. Horn. 1996. Sponsorship from management ego trip to marketing success. *Journal of Advertising Research,* July-August, 11-21.

Cronin, J., and S.A. Taylor. 1992. Measuring service quality: A re-examination and extension. *Journal of Marketing* 56, 55-68.

Crowley, M.G. 1991. Prioritising the sponsorship audience. *European Journal of Marketing* 25(11), 11-21.

Derbaix, C., and J. Brée. 2000. *Comportement du consommateur: Présentation de textes choisis.* Paris: Economica.

Derbaix, C., P. Gérard, and T. Lardinois. 1994. Essai de conceptualisation d'une activité éminement pratique: Le parrainage. *Recherche et Application en Marketing* 9(2), 41-67.

Détrie, J.P., J.P. Anastassopoulos, G. Blanc, L. Capron, M. Créladez, P. Dussauge, B. Garette, M. Ghertman, J.P. Larçon, H. Laroche, P. Lamattre, F. Leroy, B. Moingeon, J.L. Neyraut, J.P. Nioche, B. Quélin, B. Ramanantsoa, R. Reitter, M. Santi, and B. Stora. 1997. *Stratégor: Politique générale de l'entreprise.* Paris: Dunod.

Dibb, S. 2000. Market segmentation. In *The Oxford textbook of marketing,* ed. K. Blois. Oxford: Oxford University Press.

Dixon-Krauss, L. 1996. Vygotsky's sociocultural perspective on learning and its application to western literacy instruction. In *Vygotsky in the classroom: Mediated literacy instruction and assessment,* ed. L. Dixon-Krauss. White Plains, NY: Longham.

Dress, N. 1989. Sport sponsoring. PhD diss., Verlag University, Leverkusen.

Druker, P. 1990. Drucker on management: Marketing 101 for a fast changing. *The Wall Street Journal,* Nov 20, 20.

Durkeim, E. 1894. *Les règles de la méthode sociologique.* Paris: PUF.

Dussard, C. 1983. *Comportement du consommateur et stratégie de marketing.* Toronto: McGraw-Hill.

Ellwood, I. 2000. *The essential brand book: Over 100 techniques to increase brand value.* London: Kogan Page.

Engel, J.E., D.T. Kollat, and R.D. Blackwell. 1973. *Consumer behavior.* Hisdale, IL: Dryden.

Farquart, P. 1990. Managing brand equity. *Journal of Advertising Research* 30(4), 7-12.

Ferguson, N. 1981. *The human chameleon.* Hermance: Castle Publications.

Ferrand, A., and M. Nardi. In press. *Il marketing dello fitness.* Milano: Alea edizioni.

Ferrand, A., and M. Pagès. 1996. Image sponsoring: A methodology to match event and sponsor. *Journal of Sport Management* 10, 278-291.

Fishbein, M., and I. Ajzen. 1975. *Belief, attitude, intention and behavior: An introduction to theory and research.* Reading, MA: Addison-Wesley.

Fournier, S., and D.G. Mick. 1999. Rediscovering satisfaction. *Journal of Marketing* 63, 5-23.

Freeman, R.E. 1984. *Strategic management: A stakeholder approach.* Boston: Pitman.

Ganassali, S., and L. Didellon. 1996. Le transfert comme principe central du parrainage. *Recherche et Application en Marketing* 11(1), 37-48.

Giese, J.L., and J.A. Cote. 2000. Defining consumer satisfaction. *Academy of Marketing Science Review* (online), 1.

Gladden, J.M., and G.R. Milne. 1999. Examining the importance of brand equity in professional sport. *Sport Marketing Quarterly* 8(1), 21-29.

Gladden, J.M., G.R. Milne, and W.A. Sutton. 1998. A conceptual framework for assessing brand equity in Division I college. *Journal of Sport Management* 12(1), 1-19.

Gorn, G.J. 1982. The effects of music in advertising on choice behavior: A classical conditioning approach. *Journal of Marketing* 46, 94-101.

Grey, A.M., and K. Skildum-Reid. 1999. *The sponsorship seeker's toolkit.* Roseville: McGraw-Hill Australia.

Gritti, J. 1975. *Sport à la une.* Paris: Armand Colin.

Hardie, M.B., and C. Charron. 1999. The sports power shift. *Forester Research,* November.

Heider, F. 1946. Attitude and cognitive organization. *Journal of Psychology* 31, 107-113.

Holbrook, M., and E. Hirschman. 1982. The experiential aspects of consumption: Consumer fantasies, feelings, and fun. *Journal of Consumer Research* 9, 132-140.

Holden, S.J.S. 1993. Understanding brand awareness: Let me give you a C(L)Ue! *Advances in Consumer Research* 20, 383-388.

Holden, S.J.S., and R.J. Lutz. 1992. Ask not what the brand can evoke: Ask what can evoke the brand. *Advances in Consumer Research* 19, 101-107.

Hovland, C., C. Janis, and H. Kelley. 1953. *Communication and persuasion.* New Haven, CT: Yale University Press.

Hovland, C., A. Lumsdaine, and F. Sheffield. 1945. *Experiments on mass communication.* Princeton, NJ: Princeton University Press.

Howard, J.A., and J.N. Sheth. 1969. *The theory of buyer behaviour.* New York: Wiley.

Howard, S. 1989. *Corporate image management: A marketing discipline for the 21st century.* Singapore: Butterworth-Heinemann Asia.

Huizinga, J. 1951. *Homo ludens.* Paris: Gallimard.

Hustad, T.P., and E.A. Pessemier. 1974. The development and application of psychographics, life style and associated measures. In *Lifestyle and psychographics,* ed. W.D. Wells. Chicago: American Marketing Association.

Interbrand. 2003. *Brand valuation.* Dayton.

Irwin, R.L., and W.A. Sutton. 1994. Sport sponsorship objectives: An analysis of their relative importance for major corporate sponsors. *European Journal for Sport Management* 1(2), 93-101.

Jacoby, J. 1971. A model of multi-brand loyalty. *Journal of Advertising Research* 11, 25-30.

Javalgi, R.G., M.B. Traylor, A.C. Gross, and E. Lampman. 1994. Awareness of sponsorship and corporate image: An empirical investigation. *Journal of Advertising* 23(4), 47-58.

Kahle, L. 1983. *Social values and social change: Adaptation to life in America.* New York: Praeger.

Kapferer, J.N. 1988. *Les chemins de la persuasion: Le mode d'influence des média et de la publicité sur les comportements.* Paris: Dunod.

Kapferer, J.N. 1998. *Strategic brand management.* London: Kogan Page.

Kapferer, J.N., and G. Laurent. 1985. Consumer involvement profiles: A new practical approach to consumer involvement. *Journal of Advertising Research* 25(6), 48-56.

Kapferer, J.N., and G. Laurent. 1993. Further evidence in the consumer involvement profile: Five antecedents of involvement. *Psychology and Marketing* 10(4), 347-355.

Kellaris, J.J., and A.D. Cox. 1989. The effects of background music in advertising: A reassessment. *Journal of Consumer Research* 16, 113-118.

Keller, K.L. 1993. Conceptualizing, measuring, and managing customer-based brand equity. *Journal of Marketing* 57, 1-22.

Kohli, C., and L. Leuthesser. 2001. Brand equity: Capitalizing on intellectual capital. *Ivey Business Journal* 4, 3-15.

Kohli, C., and M. Thakor. 1997. Branding consumers good: Insights from theory and practice. *Journal of Consumer Marketing* 14(2-3), 306-330.

Kotler, P., M. Dubois, and D. Manceau. 2003. *Marketing management.* Paris: Pearson Education.

Lambin, J.J. 2002. *Marketing stratégique: Du marketing à l'orientation marché.* Paris: Dunod.

Lambkin, M. 2000. Strategic marketing in a modern economy. In *The Oxford textbook of marketing,* ed. K. Blois. Oxford: Oxford University Press.

Lanfranchi, P. 1996. Point de vue en: Football, ombres du spectacle. *Les Cahiers de la Sécurité Intérieure* 26, 9-17.

Learned, E.P., C.R. Christensen, K.R. Andrews, and V.D. Guth. 1965. *Business policy: Text and case.* Homewood, IL: Irwin.

Lehu, J.M. 1996. *Praximarket: Les 1000 mots clés pour maîtriser le marketing.* Paris: Jean-Pierre de Monza.

Ludwig, S., and J.D. Karabetsos. 1999. Objectives and evaluation processes utilized by sponsors of the 1996 Olympic Games. *Sport Marketing Quarterly* 8, 11-29.

Lutz, R.J. 1979. A functional theory framework for designing and pretesting advertising themes. In *Attitude research plays for high stakes,* eds. J.C. Maloney and B. Silverman. Chicago: American Marketing Association.

Maffesoli, M. 1988. *Le temps des tribus.* Paris: Méridiens Klincksieck.

Marion, G., F. Azimont, F. Mayaux, D. Michel, P. Portier, and R. Revat. 2003. *Antimanuel de marketing.* Paris: Editions d'Organisation.

Marion, G., and D. Michel. 1986. *Marketing mode d'emploi.* Paris: Editions d'Organisation.

Marthur, S. 2000. Offerings and markets: The main elements of strategic marketing decisions. In *The Oxford textbook of marketing,* ed. K. Blois. Oxford: Oxford University Press.

Martilla, J.A., and J.C. James. 1977. Importance performance analysis. *Journal of Marketing* 2, 77-79.

McDonald, C. 1991. Sponsorship and the image of the sponsor. *European Journal of Marketing* 25(11), 31-38.

McGuire, W.J. 1969. Attitudes and attitude change. In *Handbook of social psychology* (vol. 2), ed. G. Lindzey and E. Aronson. Reading, MA: Addison-Wesley.

Mediana. 2001. Olympic impact report in Slovenia, Ljubljana.

Mediana. 2002. Olympic impact report in Slovenia, Ljubljana.

Mediana. 2003. Olympic impact report in Slovenia, Ljubljana.

Meenaghan, T. 1998. Current developments and future directions in sponsorship research. *International Journal of Advertising* 17(1), 3-28.

Meenaghan, T. 1991. Sponsorship—legitimizing the medium. *European Journal of Marketing* 25(11), 5-10.

Narayana, L.L., and R.T. Markin. 1975. Consumer behaviour and product performance: An alternative conceptualisation. *Journal of Marketing,* 39,1-6.

Nicosia, F.M. 1966. *Consumer decision process: Marketing and advertising applications.* Englewood Cliffs, NJ: Prentice Hall.

Oliver, R.L. 1997. *Satisfaction: A behavioral perspective on the consumer.* New York: McGraw-Hill.

Popcorn, F., and L. Marigold. 1990. *Clicking.* London. Thorsons.

Parasuraman, A., V.A. Zeithaml, and L.L. Berry. 1988. SERVQUAL: A multiple-item scale for measuring customer perceptions of service quality. *Journal of Retailing,* spring, 12-40.

Parvatiyar, A., and J.N. Sheth. 2000. *Handbook of relationship marketing.* London: Sage.

Piquet, S. 1985. *Sponsoring.* Paris: Vuibert Gestion.

Pociello, C. 1983. *Sport et société. Approche socio-culturelle des pratiques.* Paris: Vigot.

Porter, M.E. 1980. *Competitive strategy: Techniques for analyzing industries and competitors.* New York: Free Press.

Richins, M.L. 1997. Measuring emotion in the consumption experience. *Journal of Consumer Research* 24, 127-146.

Ries, A., and J. Trout. 1981. *Positioning the battle for your mind.* New York: McGraw-Hill.

Rogge, J. 2004. Press Release. CIO. January the 5th.

Rokeach, M. 1973. *The nature of human values.* New York: Free Press.

Rosenberg, M.J., and C.I. Hovland. 1960. Cognitive, affective, and behavioral components of attitudes. In *Attitude organization and change,* ed. C.I. Hovland and M.J. Rosenberg. New Haven, CT: Yale University Press.

Ross, S. 2002. *Brand Equity in Sport: The Proposition of a New Conceptual Framework.* 2002 International Conference on Sport and Entertainment Business. Columbia, South Carolina.

Ross, S., and J. James. 2003. *Comparing sport brand associations across differing levels of identified fans.* In *Abstracts for the 18th Annual North American Society for Sport Management Conference,* Ithaca, New York, May.

Rothschild, M.L. 1984. Perspectives in involvement: Current problems and future directions. In *Advances in consumer research,* ed. T. Kinnear. Ann Arbor, MI: Association for Consumer Research.

Sahnoun, P. 1986. *Le sponsoring mode d'emploi.* Paris: Chotard et Associés.

Sandler, D., and D. Shani. 1989. Olympic sponsorship vs ambush marketing: Who gets the gold? *Journal of Advertising Research,* August-September, 9-11.

Schmitt, B.H. 1999. *Experiential marketing.* New York: Free Press.

Schmitt, B.H. 2004. *Customer experience management.* Hoboken: John Willey & Sons.

Schmitt, B.H., and A. Simonson. 1997. *Marketing aesthetics: The strategic management of brands, identity and image.* New York: Free Press.

Schwartz, S. 1992. Universals in the content and structure of values: Theoretical advance and empirical tests in 20 countries. In *Advances in experimental social psychology,* ed. M. Zanna. New York: Academic Press.

Selznick, P. 1957. *Leadership in administration: A sociological interpretation.* New York: Harper & Row.

Serraf, G. 1985. *Dictionnaire méthodologique du marketing.* Paris: Editions d'Organisation.

Shimp, T.A. 1997. *Integrated marketing communications* (4th ed.). Orlando, FL: Dryden Press.

Slater, D. 1997. *Consumer culture and modernity.* Cambridge, UK: Polity Press.

Sloan, R.L. 1989. The motives of sport fans. In *Sport games and play: Social and psychological viewpoints* (2nd ed.), ed. J.H. Goldstein. Hillsdale, NJ: Erlbaum.

Speed, R., and P. Thompson. 2000. Determinants of sports sponsorship response. *Journal of the Academy of Marketing Science* 28(2), 226-238.

Stokes, R.C. 1985. The effects of price, package design, and brand familiarity on perceived quality. In *Perceived quality: How consumers view stores and merchandise,* ed. J. Jacoby and J. Olson. Lanham, MD: Lexington Books.

Trout, J., and A. Ries. 1972. The Positioning Era Cometh. *Advertising Age,* April 24, 35-38.

Trout, J., and A. Ries. 1972. The Positioning Era Cometh. *Advertising Age,* May 1, 51-54.

Trout, J., and A. Ries. 1972. The Positioning Era Cometh. *Advertising Age,* May 8, 114-116.

Vernette, E. 1998. *Marketing mode d'emploi.* Paris: Editions d'Organisation.

Wann, D.L. 1995. Preliminary validation of the sport motivation scale. *Journal of Sport and Social Issues* 19(4), 377-396.

Wann, D.L., M.P. Schrader, and A.M. Wilson. 1999. Sport fan motivation: Questionnaire validation, comparisons by sport and relationship to athletic motivation. *Journal of Sport Behaviour,* March, 22-34.

Woodside, A.G., J.D. Clokey, and J.M. Combes. 1974. Similarities for generalized brand attitudes, behavioral intentions, and reported behaviour. *Advances in Consumer Research* 2, 34-45.

Zeithaml, V.A., and M.J. Bitner. 2003. *Service marketing: Integrating customer focus across the firm.* New York: McGraw-Hill.